Book 2

GUITAR BASICS
A Beginning Guitar Method

Second Edition

Michael Christiansen

KENDALL/HUNT PUBLISHING COMPANY
4050 Westmark Drive Dubuque, Iowa 52002

Photos by R. T. Clark

Copyright © 1986, 1993 by Michael Christiansen

ISBN 0-7872-0194-4

All rights reserved. No part of this publication may be reproduced, stored in a retrieval system, or transmitted, in any form or by any means, electronic, mechanical, photocopying, recording, or otherwise, without the prior written permission of the copyright owner.

Printed in the United States of America
10 9 8 7 6 5

Contents

    Preface v

1. **The Dead (Muted) Strum** 1
2. **Barre Chords** 5
   First Category 6
   Second Category 8
3. **Chords Over Bass Notes** 13
4. **The Chord Clock** 17
5. **Playing Single Note Melodies** 21
   Note Review 21
   Rhythm Review 22
   Key Signatures 23
   Scales 25
   Eighth Notes 26
   Eighth Rest 28
   Dotted Quarter Notes 29
   Combining Melody and Chords 30
6. **Playing Two or More Notes Together (Fingerstyle)** 33
   Rest Stroke 33
   Free Stroke 34
   Playing Two Notes Together 34
   More Than Two Notes Together 36
7. **Arpeggios** 39
8. **Playing Two or More Notes Together (Pick-Style)** 43
   Playing Two Notes Together 43
   More Than Two Notes Together 45
9. **Tablature** 47
10. **Review** 53
    Spanish Delight 53
11. **Chord Reference Sheets** 57

Preface

This book is a "follow-up" to Guitar Basics, Book I. It is assumed the student is already familiar with basic chords, strum patterns, fingerpick patterns, and the notes in first position.

Book 2 presents complex strum patterns, barre chords, melodies containing eighth notes rhythms and more than one note played at a time. While this book contains many exercises and arrangements, you may wish to supplement it with a popular songbook or sheet music to apply the material which is presented.

1
THE DEAD (Muted) STRUM

The dead strum is indicated by a strum bar with a line through it (𝄫). The chord should not be heard, but rather a sort of 'chunk' sound. The strum is done by placing the palm of the right hand over the strings and leaving the hand there while the pick (or the first finger of the right hand) strums across the strings. (See photo below.)

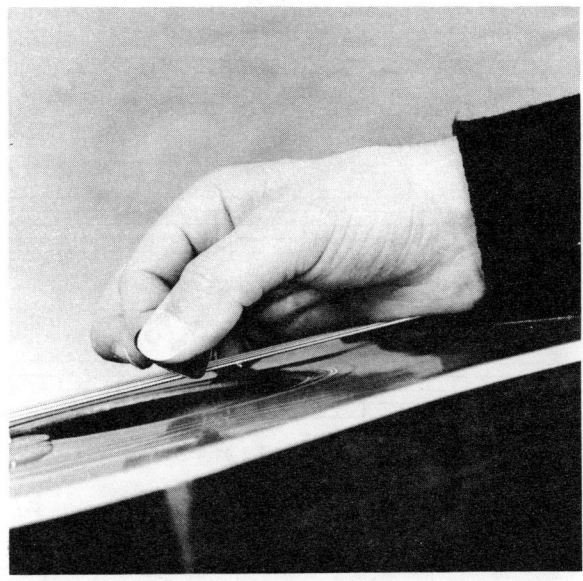

The combination of the dead strum with the clean (unmuted) strum creates some very interesting and nice accompaniment patterns. The following strum patterns may be used to play songs in 4/4. Practice the following patterns holding any chord. Make sure you feel comfortable with pattern No. 1 before doing pattern No. 2.

Pattern 1, Pattern 2, Pattern 3

Pattern 4, Pattern 5

Dead strum here

2 The Dead (Muted) Strum

Practice the following using the strum patterns on the previous page. Play the exercises using pattern 1 in each measure, then pattern 2 and so on. After playing the exercises, apply these patterns to songs in 4/4 meter from songbooks or sheet music.

If you do not know a particular chord, look it up on the Chord Reference Sheets in the back of the book (pgs. 57–60).

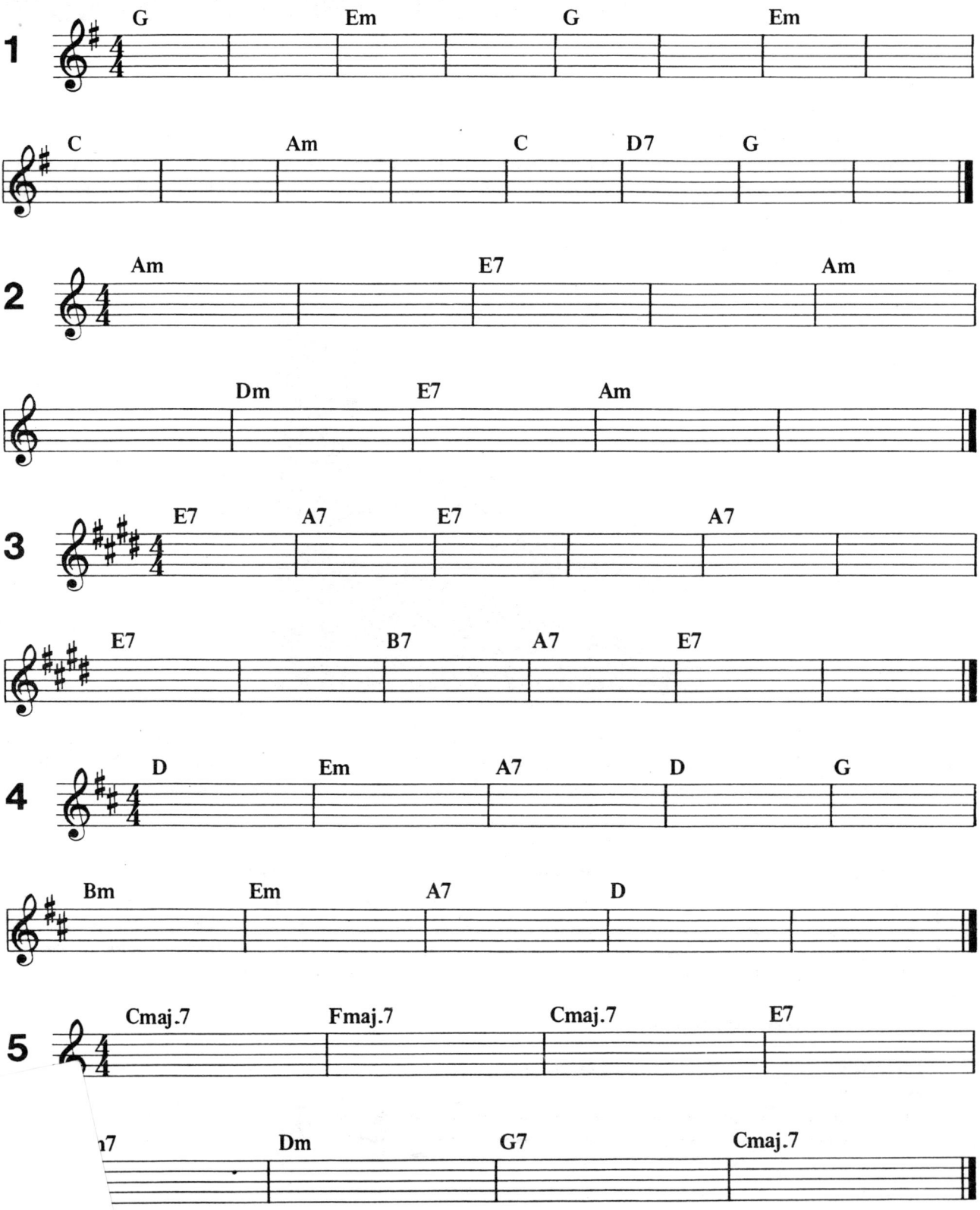

The Dead (Muted) Strum   3

If two chords appear in a measure, the patterns may be divided with the first chord getting two beats and the second chord getting two beats.

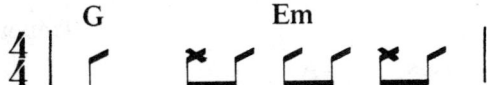

Play the following. Some measures contain two chords.

1 | D | G | Em A7 | D |

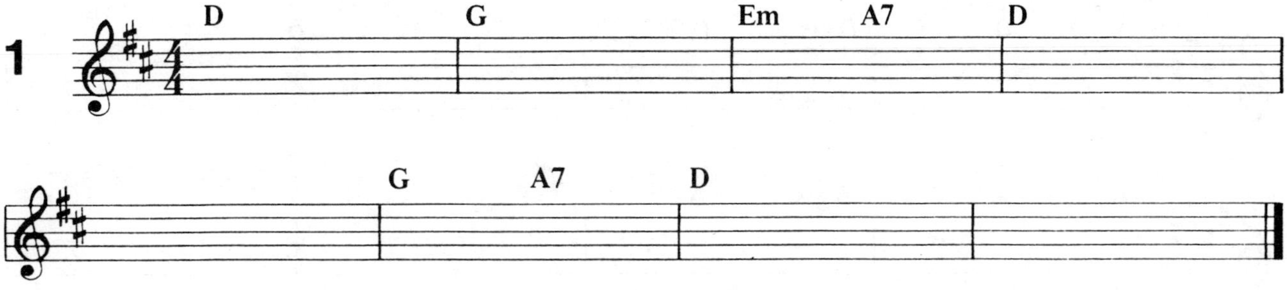

| G A7 | D ‖

2 | Em | Am Em | B7 | Em ‖

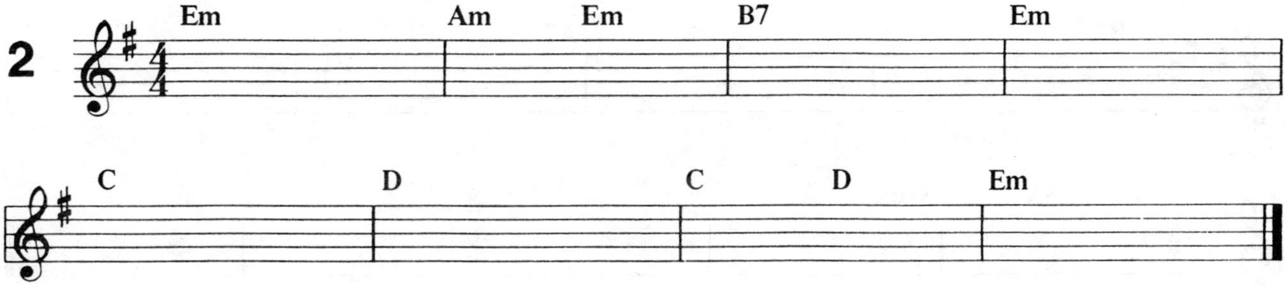

| C | D | C D | Em ‖

3 | D Dsus. D | A Asus. A G | A7sus. A7 D ‖

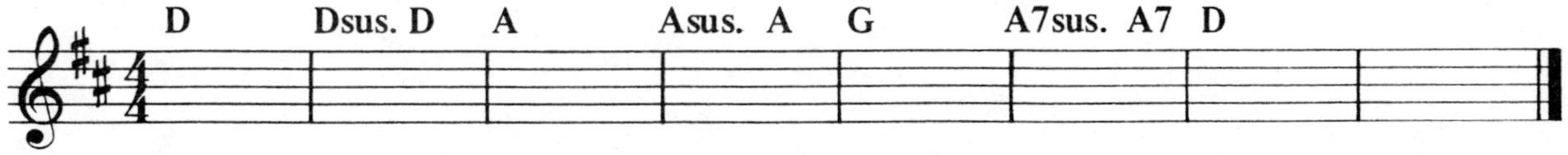

4 | G | C G D | Dsus. D ‖

| F | C G | | Cmaj.7 |

| | Am7 | D7 G ‖

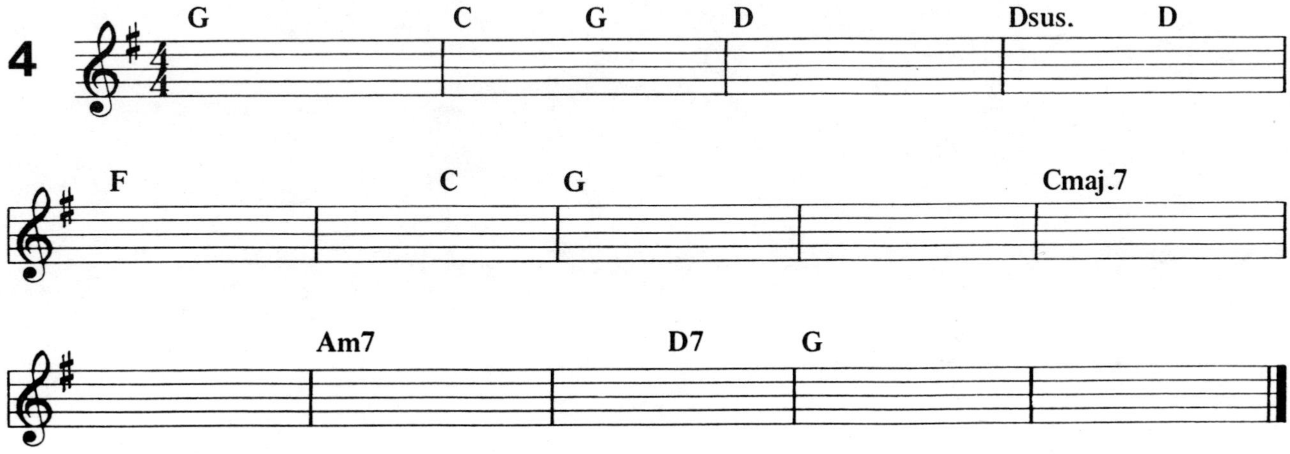

4 The Dead (Muted) Strum

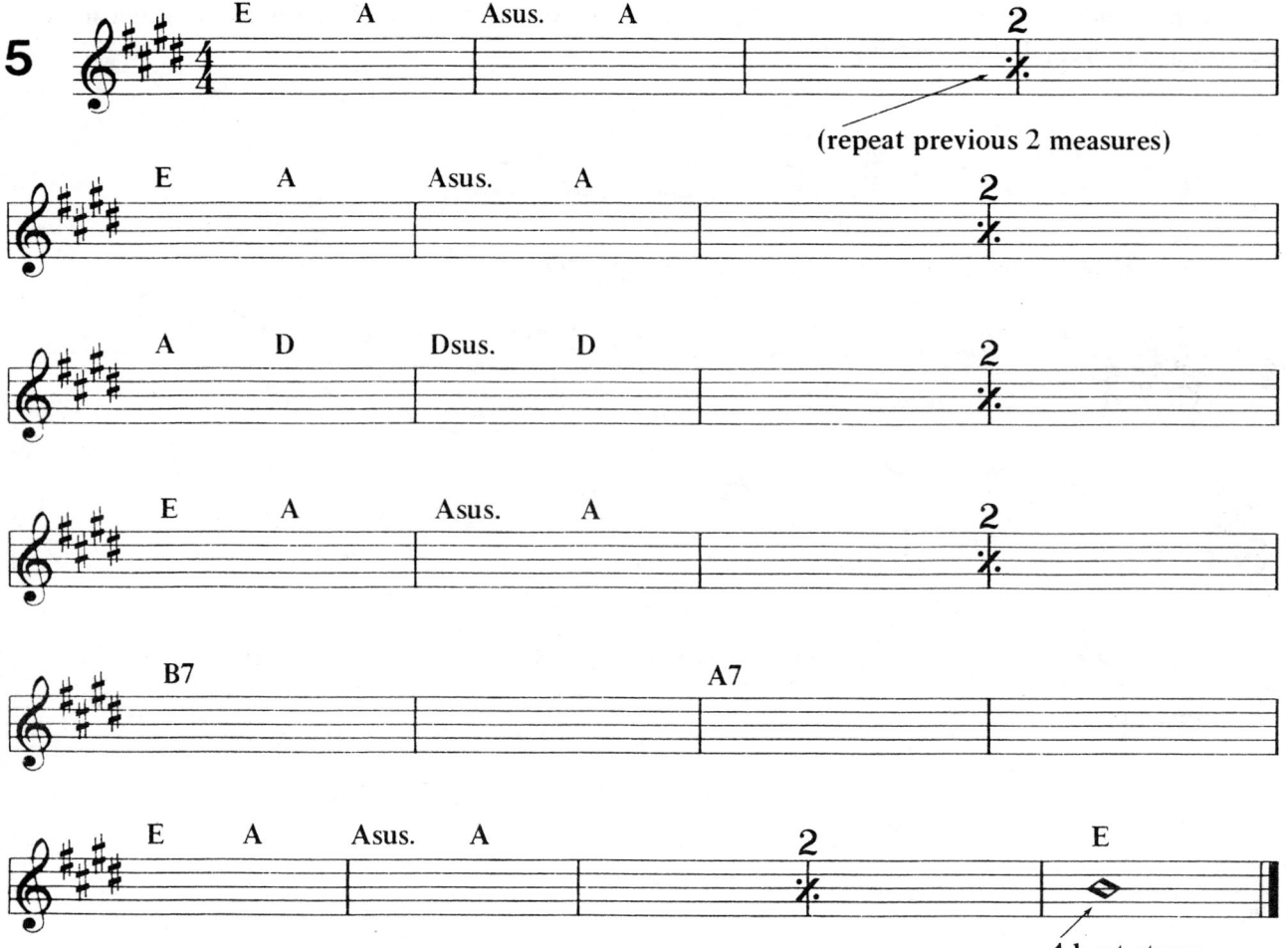

2
BARRE CHORDS

Barre chords are so called because the first finger (barre finger) lays across all of the strings. These, when mastered, make it possible to play virtually hundreds of chords with very little hand movement. By simply holding the hand in one position and moving it up and down the neck you can play 12 different chords with one finger formation or pattern. The charts on pages 6, 7, and 8 enable you to determine where and how a chord will be fingered in its barre position.

There are still many chords possible on the guitar that cannot be played in open position or in the barre chord form. However, the patterns on pages 6–8 will enable you to play many of the chords found in all styles of music.

The following is an explanation of how to use the Barre Chord Sheets:

The numbers above the letter names indicate the fret number on which the "barre finger" is to be placed. The letters tell what the name of the chord will be when the barre finger is placed in that particular fret number. The various patterns illustrate how the different types of chords should be fingered after the correct fret for the barre finger has been determined.

For example, suppose you wanted to find an F chord. With the first category, the F is played with the barre finger in the first fret and the formation for the Major chord should be used. If you want to find a G7 using the first category, it is played with the barre finger in the third fret and the formation for the 7th should be used.

Remember the Major chords are those with simple letter names. They may be followed by a "sharp" sign (♯) or a "flat" sign (♭), but they will have no other letters or numbers following the basic chord name (see p. 57). This is a sharp sign ♯. If it follows a chord name, that chord is sharped. For example, an F sharp chord is written "F♯." This is a flat sign ♭. If it follows a chord letter, that chord is flatted. For example, a B flat chord is written B♭. To sharp a barre chord move the complete pattern up one fret. To flat a chord, move the complete pattern down one fret.

6 Barre Chords

FIRST CATEGORY

| 1 | 3 | 5 | 7 | 8 | 10 | 12 | —The fret number in which the barre finger is placed. |
| F | G | A | B | C | D | E | —The chord name |

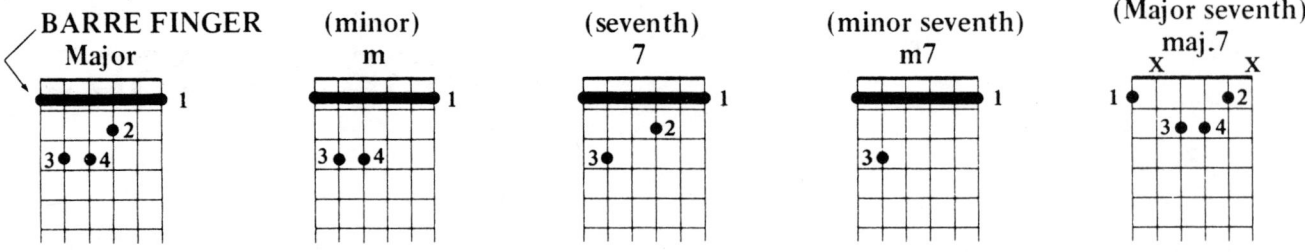

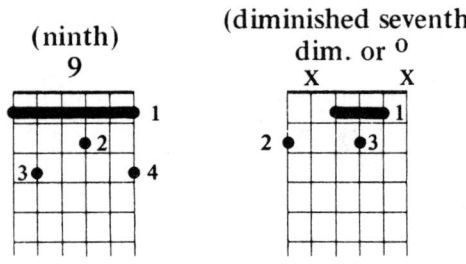

In the case that there is no barre finger used in this group of patterns, the finger on the 6th or 1st string will determine the fret number naming the chord. "X" above a string indicates that string is to be muted while strumming the chord.

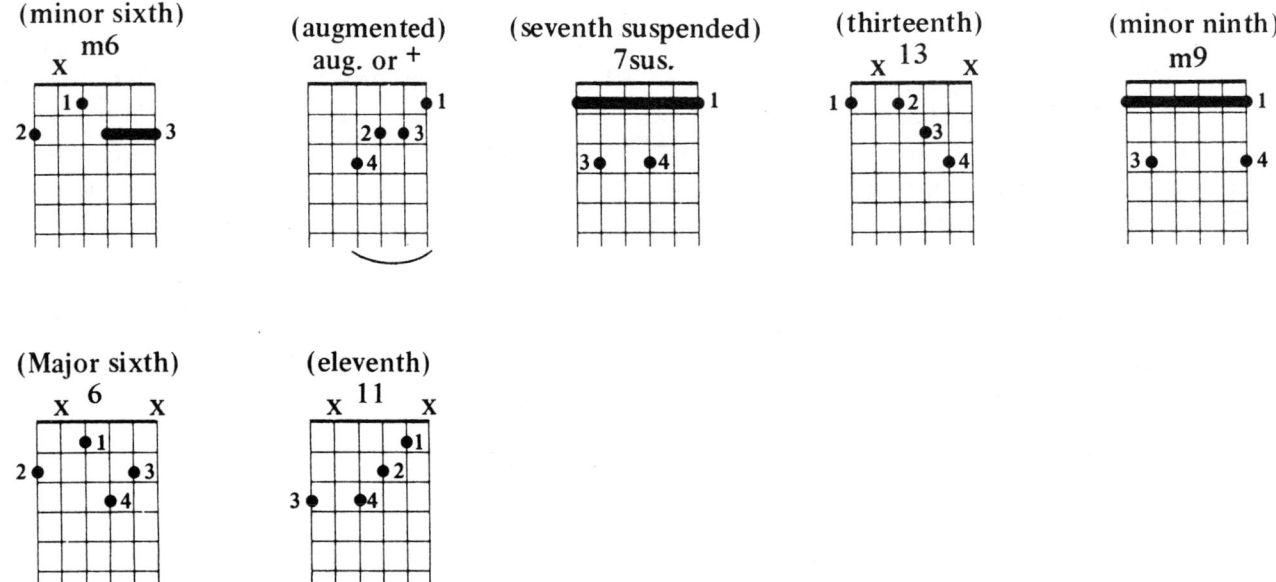

*The fingerings for some of the chords found on this page, and in the second category of barre chords, do not have a finger which barres across the strings. These are called 'dead string' chords. The string with the x above it is to be muted (or deadened). This is done by tilting a finger which is pushing on a lower string and lightly touching the string which is to be muted. If the chord is strummed, the muted string should not be heard.

Barre Chords

Practice the following using barre chords from the first category (p. 6). The exercises may be strummed or fingerpicked. The chords in the first category of barre chords are 6-string chords. Play all of the chords in the exercises as barre chords.

8   Barre Chords

SECOND CATEGORY

| 2 | 3 | 5 | 7 | 8 | 10 | 12 | —The fret number in which the barre finger is placed. |
| B | C | D | E | F | G | A | —The chord name |

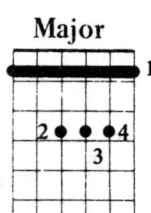
Major

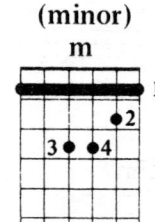
(minor)
m

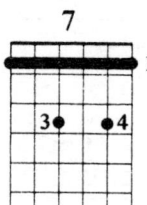
7

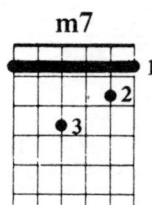
m7

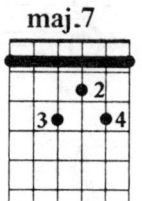
maj.7

In the case that there is no barre finger used in this group of patterns the finger on the 5th string will determine the fret number naming the chord.

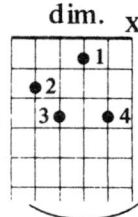
dim. x

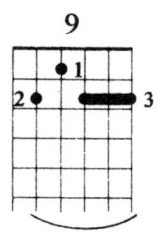
9

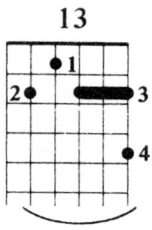
13

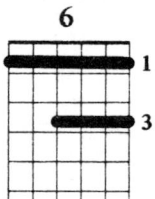
6

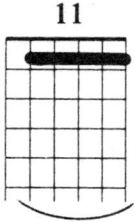
11

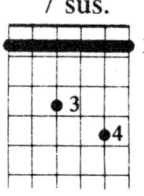
7 sus.

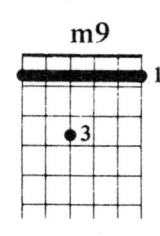
m9

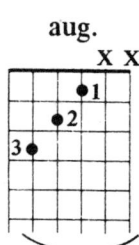
aug.
x x

Practice the following using barre chords from the second category (p. 8). If you fingerpick, barre chords from the second category should be played as 5-string chords. Play all of the chords as barre chords.

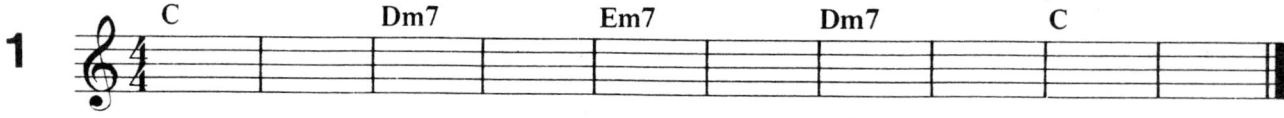
1   C   Dm7   Em7   Dm7   C

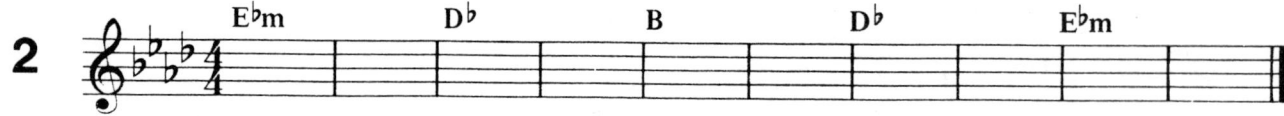
2   E♭m   D♭   B   D♭   E♭m

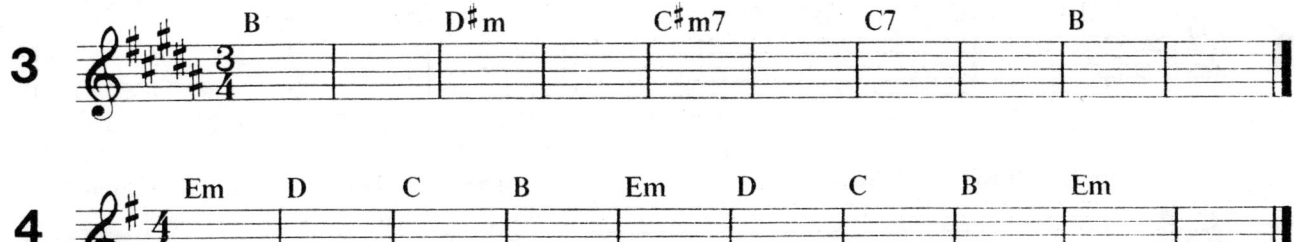

C♯m7 should be played in the ninth fret with the first category since the C chords are found in the 8th fret. C♯m7 may also be played in the fourth fret using the second category and playing the m7 pattern (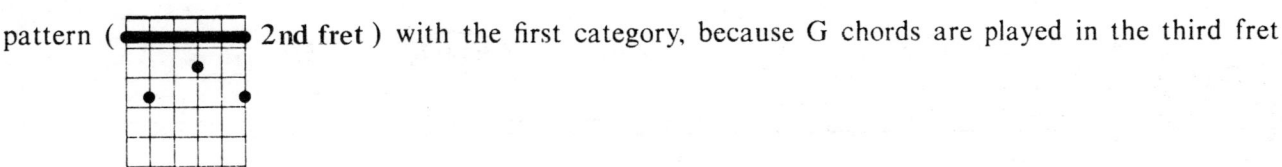 4th fret). Gb9 may be played with the barre finger in the 2nd fret and the 9th pattern (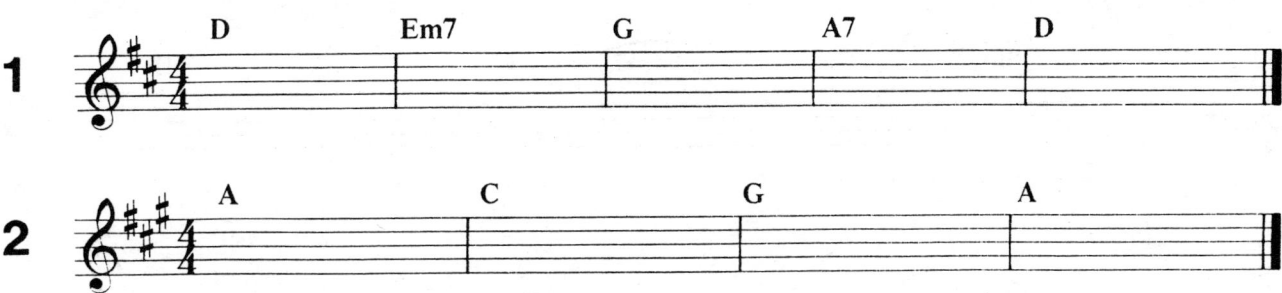 2nd fret) with the first category, because G chords are played in the third fret and you move a chord down one fret to flat it. It (Gb9) may also be played in the ninth fret and the other 9th pattern ( ) using the second category. There are two different fingerings and positions to play the same barre chord. This makes changing chords more convenient.

For example, if you are playing a piece with changes from a G to a C rapidly, one would not play a G in the third fret and a C in the eighth fret using the same pattern. This would be too awkward. It would be better to play G in the third fret and C in the 3rd fret using the other category. This would make it possible to change much faster than G to C. So you see it is possible to figure out a possible 324 different chords using the barre chord sheets correctly.

Practice the following using barre chords from both the first and second categories. You may have to figure out two ways to play the same chord and then choose the one which is closest to the chord you are already playing.

Barre Chords

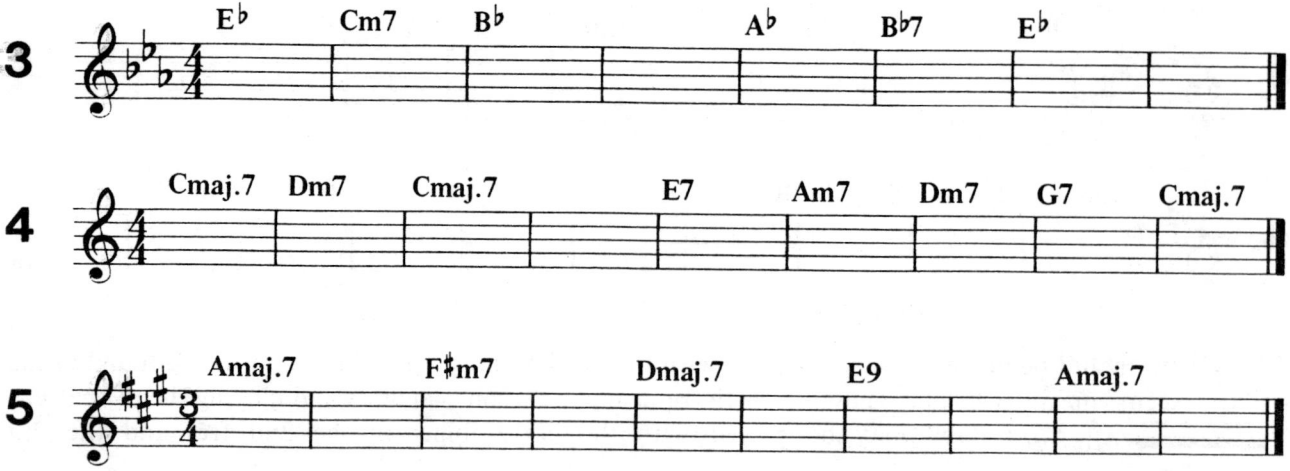

When strumming barre chords, all of the strings may be strummed. Try strumming the following piece with a few barre chords. The circled chords should be played as barre chords.

Try strumming the following:

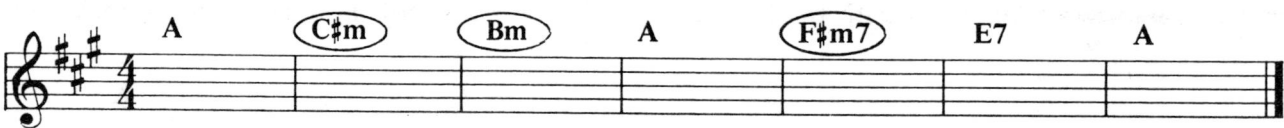

Notice how full and rich the barre chords sound compared to some of the open chords, because of the fact that all of the strings are being strummed. Try the following example and keep in mind that one wouldn't go from G in the third fret to Bm in the 7th, but rather G in the third fret to Bm in the second fret.

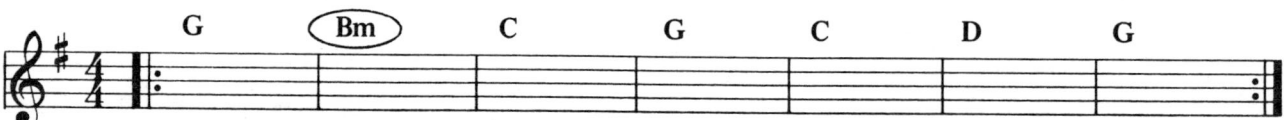

Fingerpick or strum the following examples playing the circled chords as barre chords. If barre chords are fingerpicked, the chords in the second category are 5-string chords and the chords in the first category are 6-string chords.

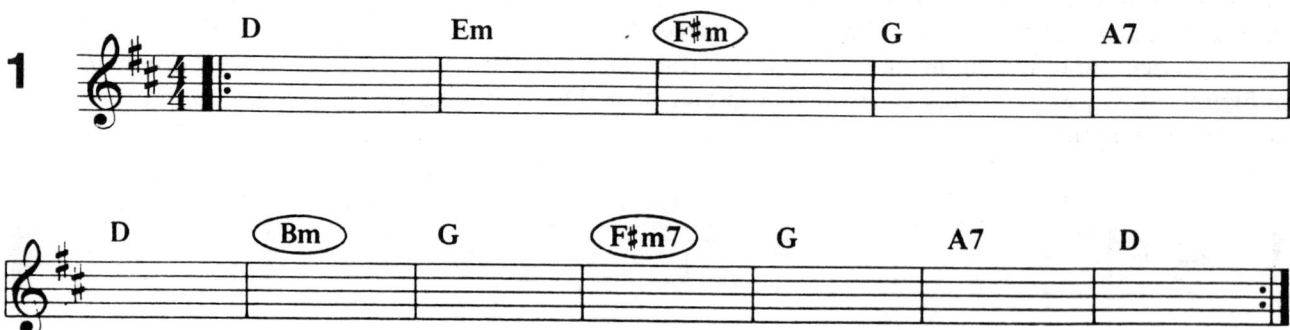

Barre Chords 11

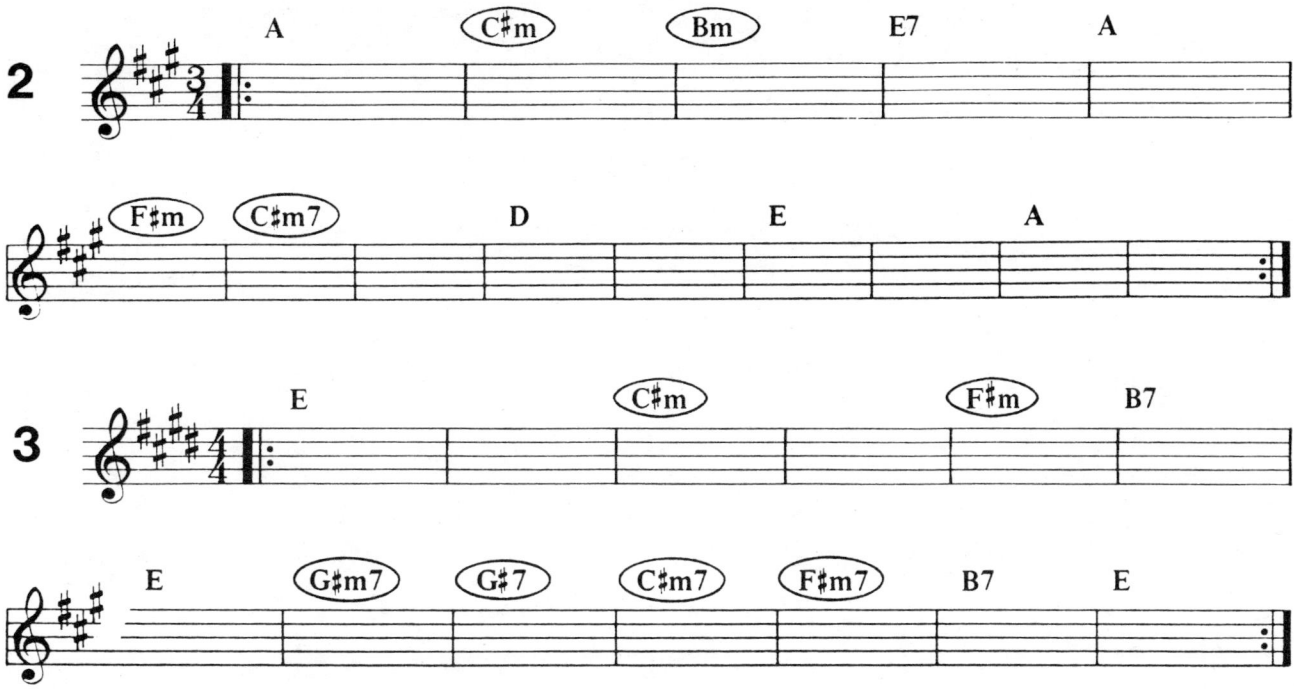

Practice strumming following blues progressions using barre chords from both categories. Play all of the chords as barre chords.

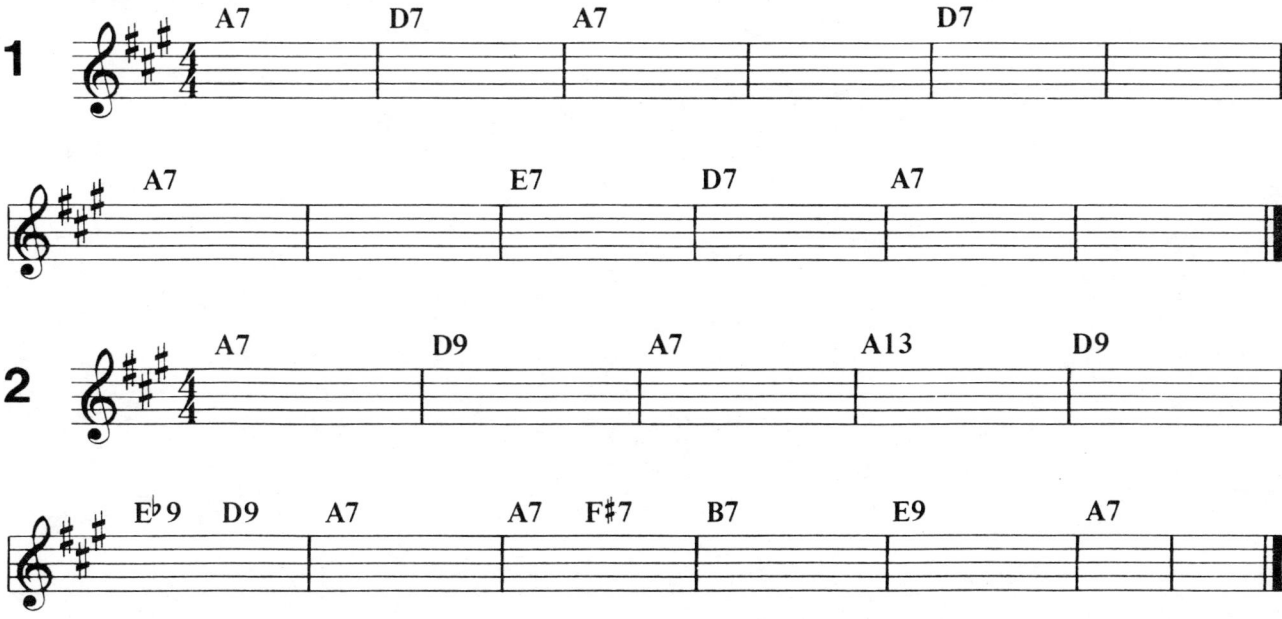

Practice songs from sheet music or songbooks playing some of the chords as barre chords. A chord should be played as a barre chord if it is sharp or flat and if there is not a way to play it as an open chord.

3
CHORDS OVER BASS NOTES

Occasionally chords such as D/C will appear. D/C means a D chord with a C note in the bass, or the lowest note to be played is C. It is ONE chord name. It is fingered thus: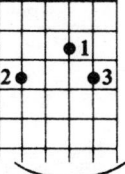

These chords have an unusual sound when strummed, but if the proper fingerpick, or alternating bass pattern, is used they add a very interesting effect.

These are some of the more popular chords over bass notes. Try holding the following chords.

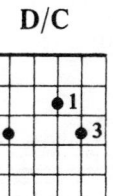 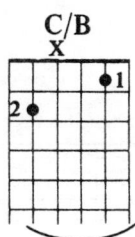 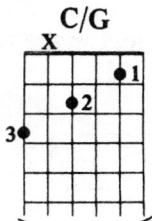 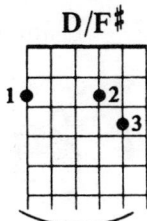

D/C   C/B   C/G   D/F♯

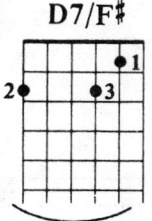 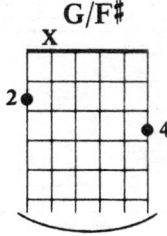 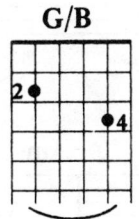 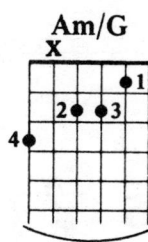

D7/F♯   G/F♯   G/B   Am/G

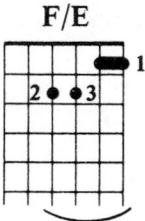 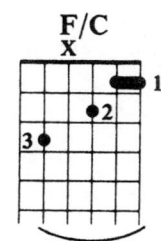

F/E   F/C

Chords Over Bass Notes

Try playing the following exercises using chords over bass notes. The fingerpick patterns, or alternating bass patterns may be used. Special fingerpick patterns for the chords over bass notes are indicated in the measures.

Try the following using the Travis pick style:

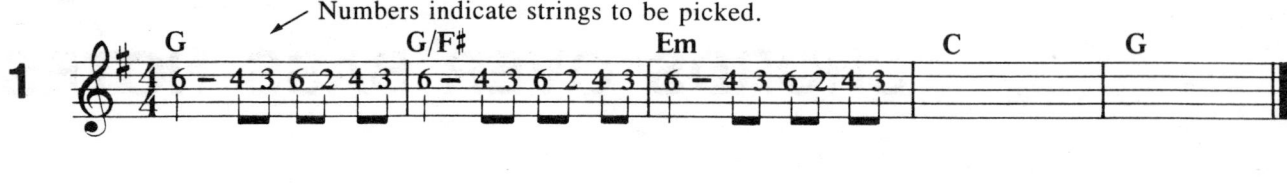

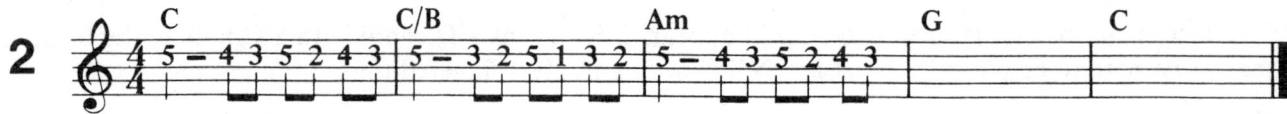

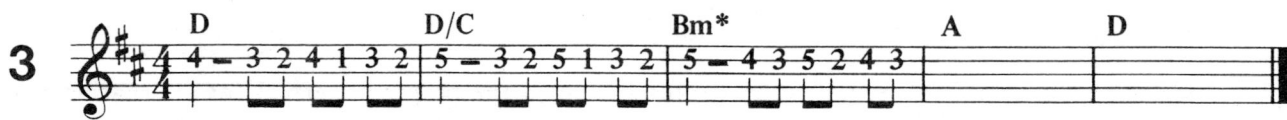

*The barre chord Bm would sound better here. See the section on barre chords. Notice that the fingerpick patterns have been modified on some of the chords with added bass notes. For example: C/B.

Using the Travis pick style, try the following examples:

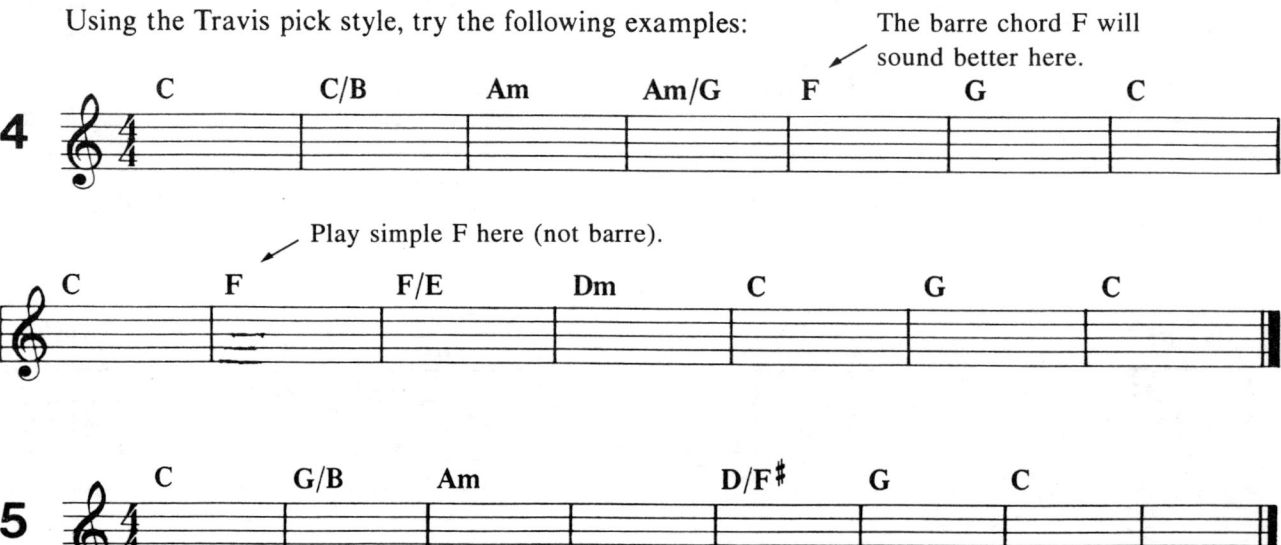

Chords Over Bass Notes 15

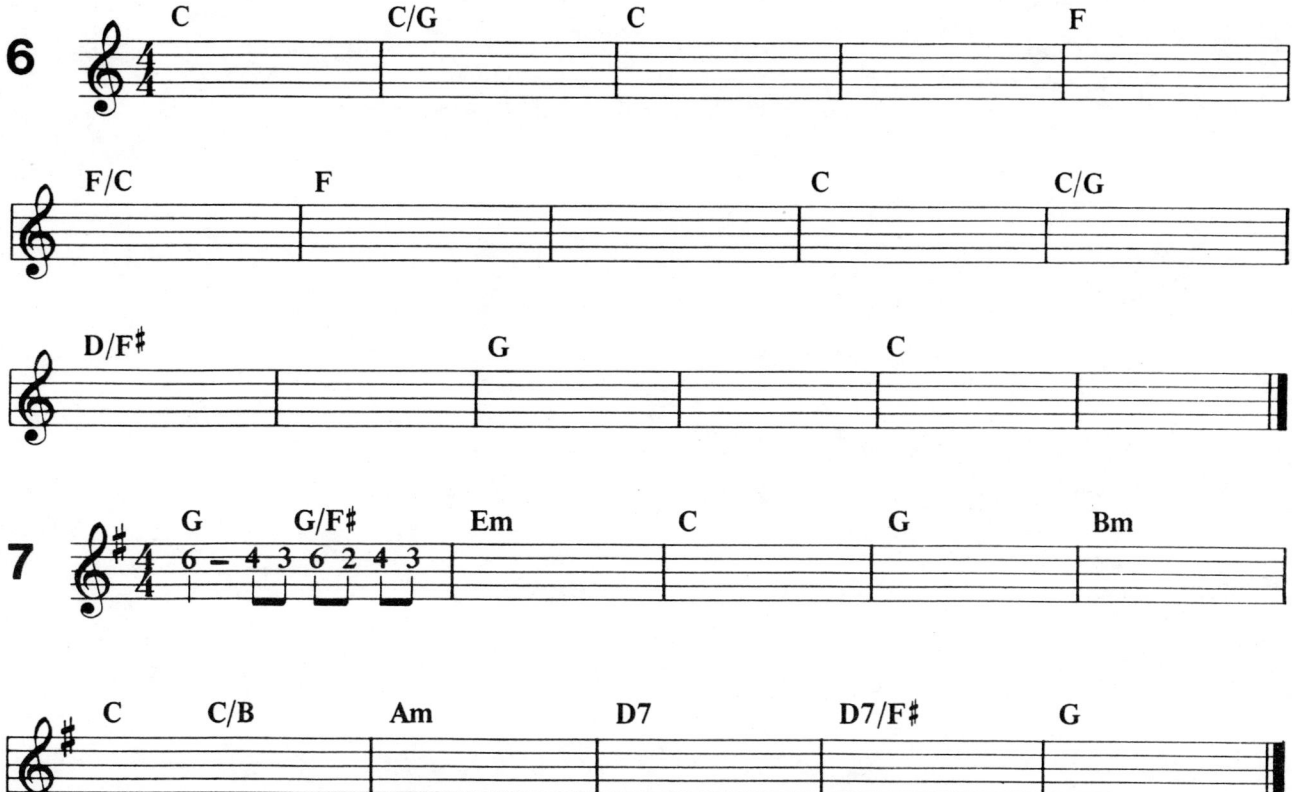

4
THE CHORD CLOCK (Circle of Fifths)

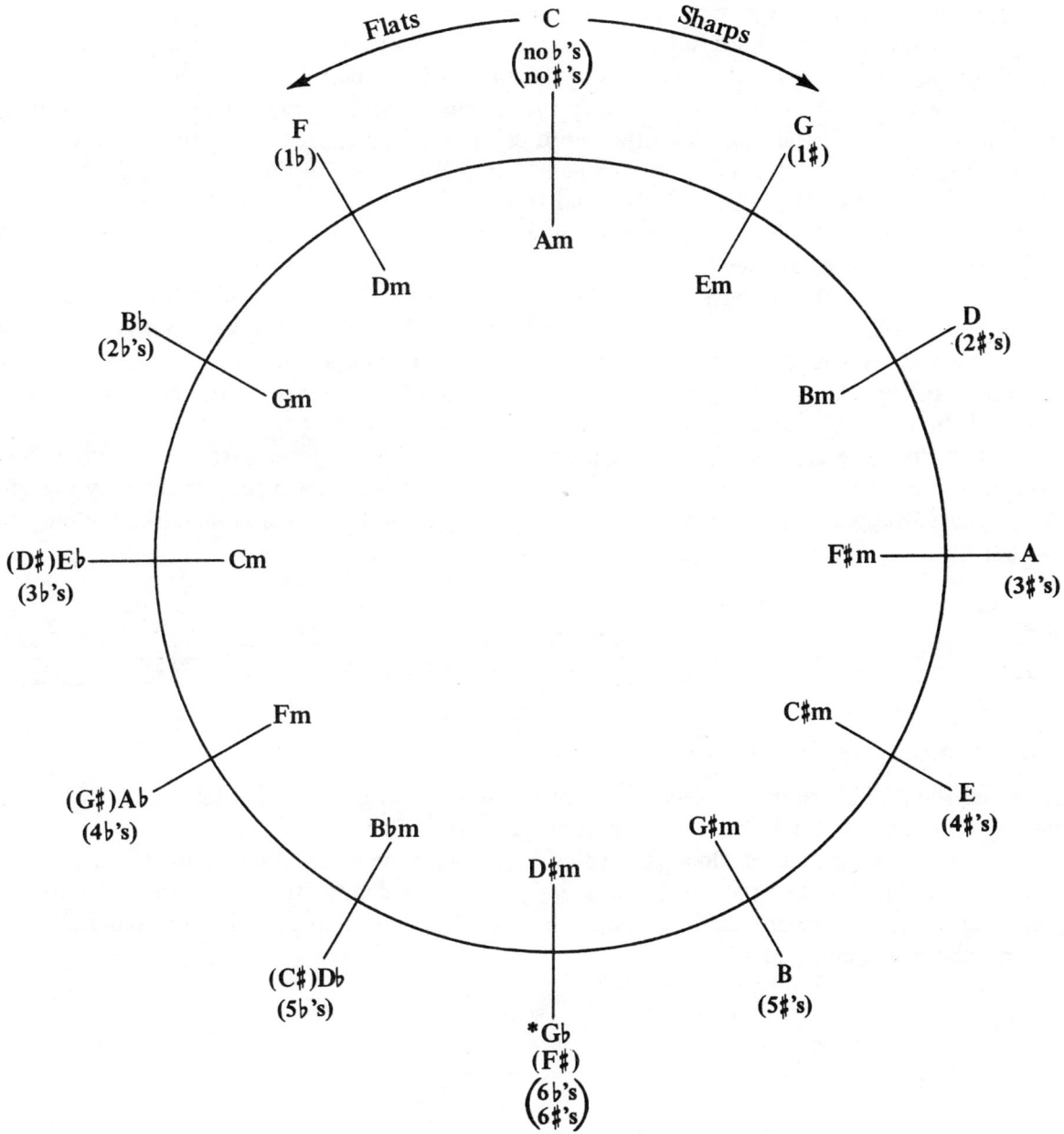

This is a chord clock. It can be used in three ways:

1. It can be used to determine the number of sharps or flats in a given key.
2. It can be used to determine the basic chords in a key.
3. It can be used to transpose music. This means to change the key.

The Chord Clock

You can determine the key of a particular piece by looking at the key signature. The key signature is the sharps or flats found at the beginning of each staff. The number of sharps or flats in the key signature determines the key in which the piece is written. If a piece has one or more sharps in its key signature, it will be in one of the keys on the right half of the chord clock. If a piece has one or more flats in its signature, it will be in one of the keys on the left half of the clock. For example, the key of C or Am will have no sharps or flats in its key signature. The key of G or Em will have one sharp sign in its signature, the key of D or Bm will have two sharps in its signature, the key of A or F♯m will have three sharps in its signature, etc. The key of F or Dm will have one flat in the signature, the key of B♭ or Gm will have two flats in the signature, the key of E♭ or Cm will have three flats, etc.

You can determine the six basic chords in a given key by also using the chord clock. To find the basic chords in a key, take the chord having the name of the key (key chord) and the first chords to the right and to the left of it. Those three chords and their related chords (chords on the inside of the clock will correspond with the outside chords) make up the six basic chords in any given key. For example, to find the chords in the key of G, find G on the chord clock. Use the chords to the right and left of it (C and D) and their related chords (A minor, B minor, E minor) to give you the six basic chords in the key of G. The chords would be G, C, D, Am, Em, and Bm.

This process can be very helpful to the person who wants to play a piece by ear. If you want to play "Down in the Valley" without the use of music, choose the key you want to use. For instance, use the key of G. You know that the six basic chords for that key are G, C, D, Am, Em, Bm. Start by singing the melody and strumming a G chord (most simple folk songs begin with the key chord); then, when it sounds like the melody you are singing conflicts with the chord you are playing, change to one of the other chords in the key. If you change to a chord that still conflicts, change to another chord in the key until you find the one that sounds correct.

The chord clock can also be used to transpose (change the key). The easiest keys for the guitar are G, C, and D and Em, Am, and Bm. If you want to make the chords in a piece simple, play the song in one of these keys. Suppose a piece is written in a different key and the chords look like the ones in the example below:

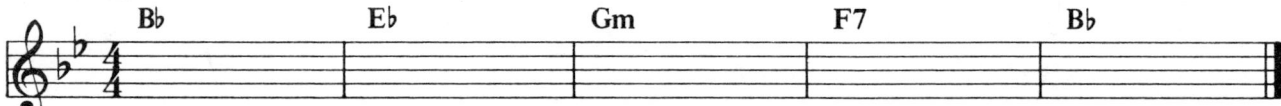

These chords can be transposed and made simple by:

1. Changing the first chord in the piece to one of the simple key chords (G, C, D, etc.)
2. Finding on the chord clock the original first chord in the piece.
3. Finding the new chord on the clock that you are changing the original chord to.
4. Seeing which direction and the number of steps you went to change the old chord to the new chord.
5. Changing the rest of the chords in the piece the same number of steps and in the same direction as the first chord was changed.

Example

Change the Bb chord to a G chord. Then, find Bb on the clock and notice that we had to go four steps (counting the Bb chord as ♮) clockwise to get to a G chord. Now, we change the rest of the chords in the piece four steps clockwise. Notice that the number of steps and the direction you change the first chord in the piece will determine the number of steps and the direction you change the rest of the chords. Shown below are the original chords and the new chords to the example:

G ← new	C	Em	D7	G
Bb key	Eb	Gm	F7	Bb

The minor chords will change the same direction and number of steps but will remain on the inside of the clock. To transpose 7th chords such as the F7 in the example, find F on the clock, change it to the new chord (D), then, add the 7th to the chord name. The F7 is changed to a D7. The same principle applies to m7, 9, 13, and other various chords.

5

PLAYING SINGLE NOTE MELODIES

NOTE REVIEW

These are the notes in first position and the higher notes on the first string. The circled number below the note is the string number on which the note is found. The numbers above are fret numbers. The letter name of the note is written to the right.

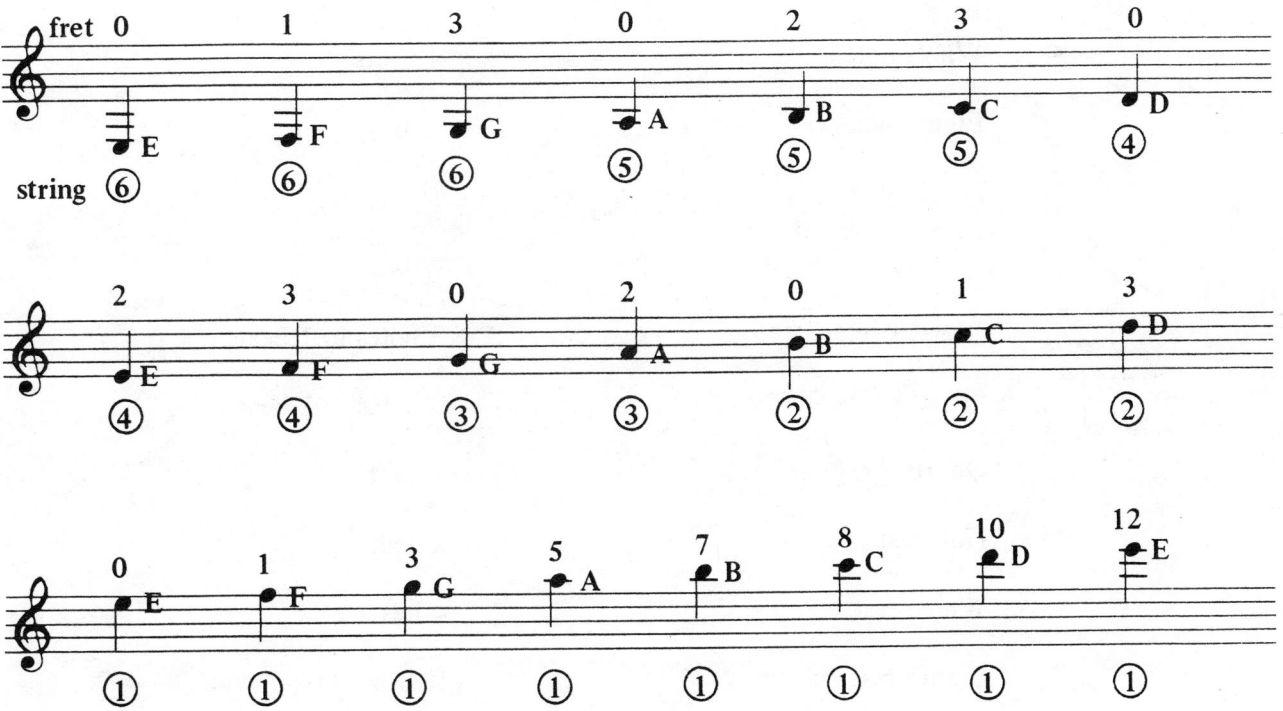

Remember: To sharp a note (♯), move it up one fret; to flat a note (♭), move it down one fret. A natural sign (♮) cancels a sharp or flat.

21

RHYTHM REVIEW

The following time values of the notes are given assuming that the bottom number of the time signature in the music is 4. The quarter note would get the basic unit or one beat. If the bottom number of the time signature were 8, then the eighth note would get one beat and the time values of the following notes would be double.

	NAME	TIME VALUE
♩	Quarter Note.	1 beat
♩	Half note—pick the note on the 1st beat and let it sound through the 2nd beat.	2 beats
♩.	Dotted half note. The dot increases the length of the note by ½ its original time value.	3 beats
o	Whole note	4 beats
♪	Eighth note	½ beat
♩.	Dotted quarter note	1½ beats
♬	16th note	¼ beat
♪♪♪	1 beat triplet	3 notes to 1 beat
♩♩♩	2 beat triplet	3 notes to 2 beats
𝄽	Quarter rest	1 beat
𝄼	Half rest	2 beats
𝄻	Whole rest	4 beats
𝄾	Eighth rest	½ beat

Playing Single Note Melodies 23

KEY SIGNATURES

Sharp, flat, and natural signs are referred to as *accidentals*.

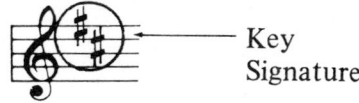 — Key Signature

The *Key Signature* is the sharps or flats which appear at the beginning of each staff. The key signature indicates which notes to sharp or flat throughout the entire piece. The names of the lines and spaces on which the sharps or flats are written in the key signature indicate which notes to sharp or flat throughout the piece. In the key signature shown above, all of the F's and C's would be sharped. A natural sign (♮) cancels a sharp or flat and is effective throughout that measure.

Play the following being sure to sharp or flat the notes indicated in the key signature. You may use a pick or the first two fingers of the right hand to play the notes.

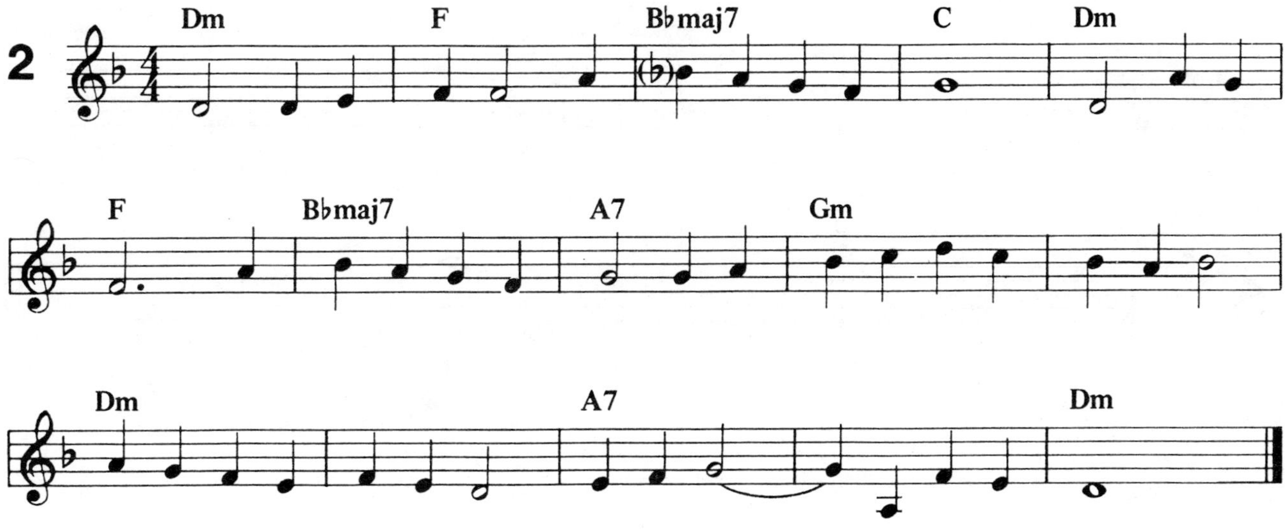

24 Playing Single Note Melodies

SCALES

Practice the following major and minor scales. Master one before going on to the next. Use them to supplement the rest of the material in this book. Notice the key signatures for each scale. The letter names tell the names of the scale and of the key.

Major Scales

Natural Minor Scales

A harmonic minor (raised 7th step)   A melodic minor. Raised 6th and 7th steps ascending. Natural 6th and 7th steps descending.

26 Playing Single Note Melodies

EIGHTH NOTES

This section is written for the guitarists using a 'pick.' However, fingerstyle players could play the exercises and pieces alternating fingers i and m.

♪ This is an eighth note. It gets ½ beat if the bottom number in the time signature is 4. Two of them connected ♫ equal one beat. If two eighth notes are connected together, the second one is counted as "and."

Example:

count: 1 & 2 & 3 & 4 & 1 2 & 3 & 4

If a pick is used, it is important to stroke the first eighth note down and the second one up.

If you are tapping your foot on the beat, the first eighth note is picked when your foot is down and the second one picked when your foot is up. Play the following containing eighth notes. Count out loud and tap your foot.

Strum a G chord one time

Playing Single Note Melodies 27

Arkansas Traveller
Anon.

Playing Single Note Melodies

Turkey in the Straw
Anon.

The name of this note is A. It is played on the first string 5th fret.

EIGHTH REST

𝄾 This is an eighth rest. When it appears, rest for ½ beat.

Emily's Frolic

Play the following containing the eighth rest.

Playing Single Note Melodies

DOTTED QUARTER NOTES

♩. The dot behind the note lengthens the time value of the note by ½ its original value. The dotted quarter note would get 1½ beats.

Play the following containing dotted quarter notes. *Watch the key signature.*

Michael Row the Boat Ashore

Exercise 33

Kum Ba Yah

Playing Single Note Melodies

Silent Night

COMBINING MELODY AND CHORDS

When a strum sign  appears in the following pieces, strum whichever chord is written above the measure down one time. The strum gets one beat. Make the strums softer than the melody. In the case there is no chord name above the measure, play whichever chord was written above the preceding measure.

The following arrangements are to be played with a pick rather than fingerstyle.

Wildwood Flower *Bluegrass Song*

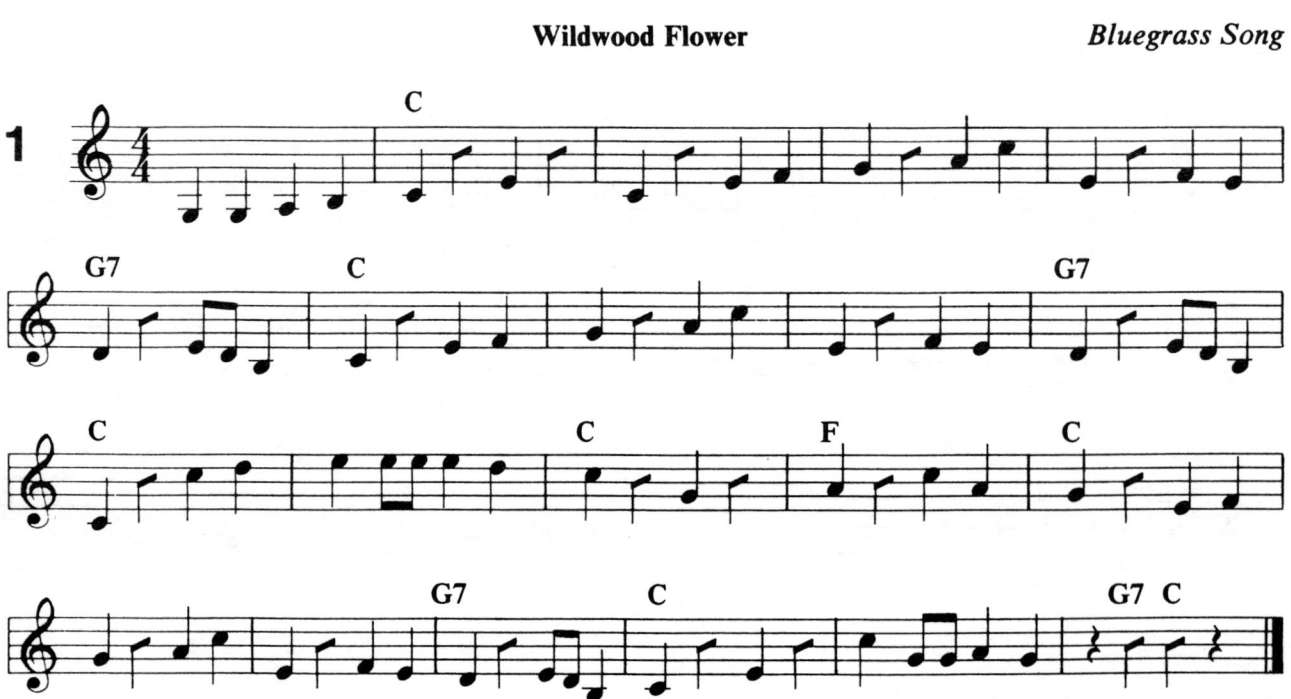

Playing Single Note Melodies 31

Amazing Grace
Anon.

two beat strum

Melody for Kathy

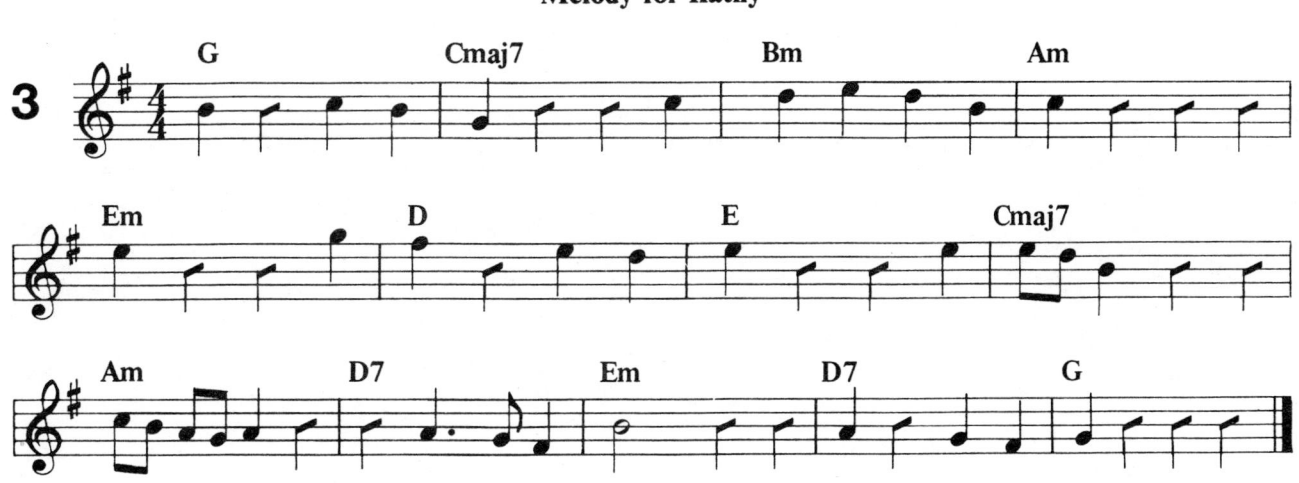

6
PLAYING TWO OR MORE NOTES TOGETHER (Fingerstyle)

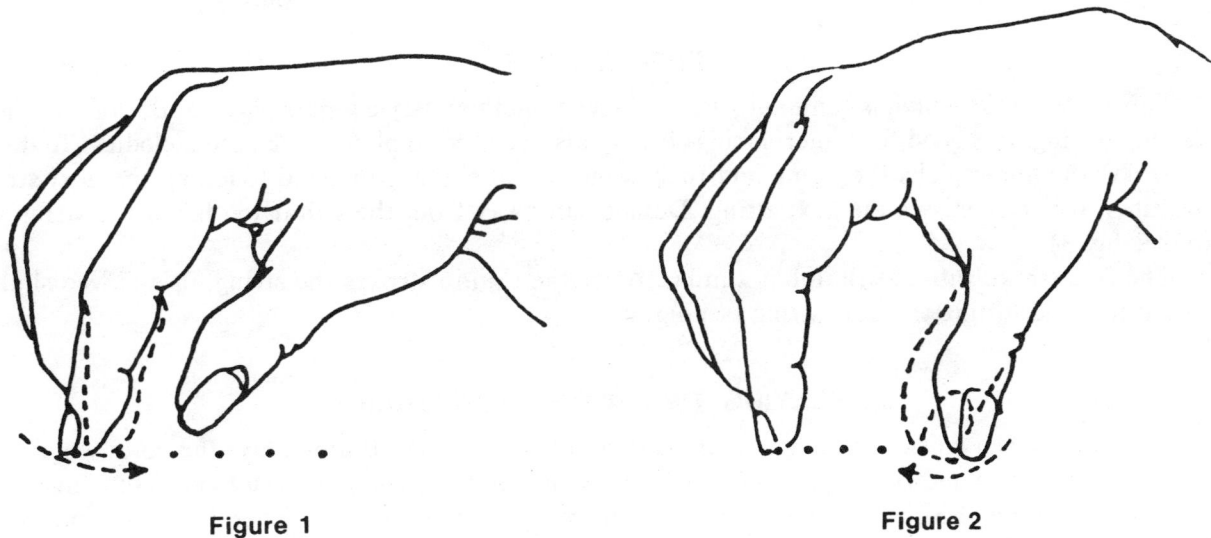

Figure 1   Figure 2

REST STROKE

The rest stroke is commonly used to play melodies and is popular in solo guitar playing. To do the rest stroke, the flesh on the tip of the finger strokes the string in an upward (not outward) motion. The nail strokes the string as it passes by. The finger then comes to rest on the next string (see fig. 1).

The thumb rest stroke is done by moving the thumb downward and playing the string with the tip of the thumb and the nail. The thumb then comes to rest on the next string down (see fig. 2).

34 Playing Two or More Notes Together (Fingerstyle)

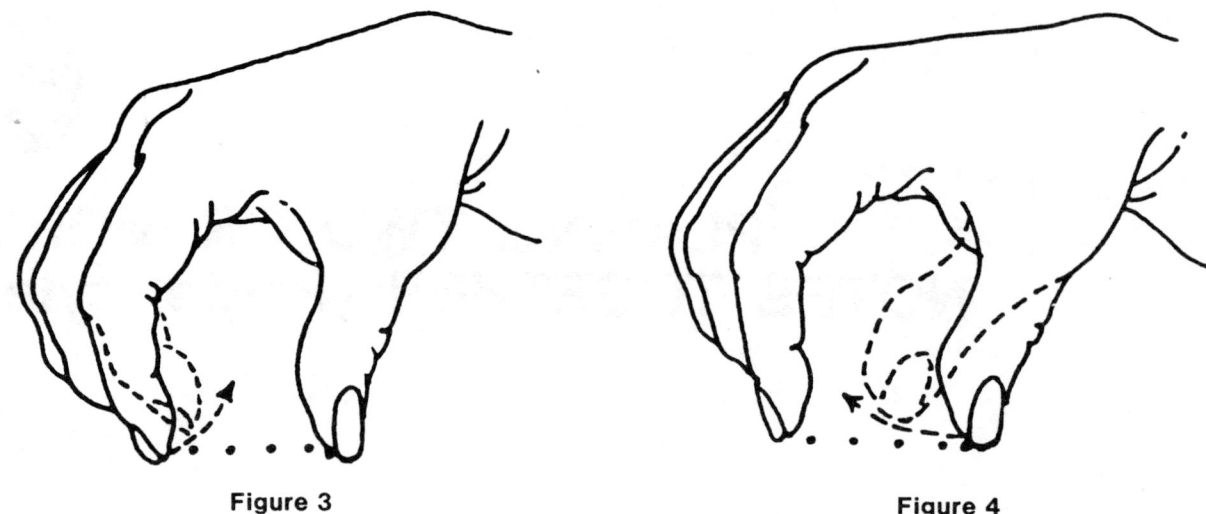

Figure 3　　　　　　　　　　Figure 4

FREE STROKE

This is the stroke which is commonly used in accompaniment style guitar playing. Because it allows the string to ring, it is good for fingerpicking. It may also be used to play single note melodies. To do the free stroke, the finger picks the string and then is pulled out slightly to avoid touching the next string. Remember, it barely misses the next string. Do not pull away from the guitar too far or the string will slap (see fig. 3).

The free stroke with the thumb is similar. After the thumb strokes the string, it is moved slightly outward to avoid hitting the next string (see fig. 4).

PLAYING TWO NOTES TOGETHER

Generally, when music for the guitar is written in two parts, the thumb plays the notes which have the stems going down and the fingers play the notes with the stems going up. Each part (the fingers and the thumb) contains the correct number of beats to complete the measure. Therefore, the thumb part may have a rest while the fingers are playing and visa versa.

Play the following using a free stroke with the thumb and a rest stroke with the fingers (see rest and free stroke descriptions). The letters above or below the notes indicate which right-hand finger should be used to stroke the string.

Playing Two or More Notes Together (Fingerstyle)

Play the following arrangement of Greensleeves. Be sure to hold the bass note (low note) for its total time value. A finger may have to be holding a bass note and allowing it to ring while the melody (upper notes) is moving.

Letters by the notes indicate which right hand finger to use when picking the string. Numbers indicate left hand fingers and a circled number indicates the string on which that note is to be played.

Greensleeves

36 Playing Two or More Notes Together (Fingerstyle)

MORE THAN TWO NOTES TOGETHER

If three notes appear on top of one another, use the thumb to play the bottom note and the fingers to play the top notes. Generally, the first two fingers, (i, m) on the right hand are used. However, you may want to check fingerings if they are indicated differently on the music.

Play the following arrangements of Españoleta #1 and Jesu, Joy of Man's Desiring which contain more than two notes played together.

Españoleta #1 — G. Sanz

Playing Two or More Notes Together (Fingerstyle) 37

This ♪♪♪ is an eighth note triplet. Three notes are played in one beat. They are counted: one-trip-let, two-trip-let, etc.

Jesu, Joy of Man's Desiring — J. S. Bach

7
ARPEGGIOS

When the notes of a chord are played one after another rather than simultaneously, this is called an "arpeggio." Arpeggios can sometimes be spotted by finding a series of notes which are evenly spaced. Such as:

When playing an arpeggio, find the series of notes and place fingers (if necessary) on them. Play the notes one after another allowing each note to sound through the arpeggio. Be sure to analyze the placement of each note in the arpeggio. The thumb and the fingers should play using the free stroke so the strings may ring.

Play the following using arpeggios:

Arpeggios

Arpeggios

Estudio

D. Aquado
arr. Aaron Shearer

*Play the B note on the 3rd string in the 4th fret. Remember, the circled number indicates on which string the note is to be played. The other numbers are suggested left hand fingerings.

8

PLAYING TWO OR MORE NOTES TOGETHER (Pick-Style)

This section of the book is to be played using a pick.

PLAYING TWO NOTES TOGETHER

When two notes are written on top of one another, they are to be played at the same time. This is called *two part harmony*. To play two notes together, first, find where the *top* note is played on the guitar, then find where the bottom note is on the guitar and play both notes together. The pick should strike both strings quickly so they sound at the same time.

For example: ♩ = 1 beat ♩ = 1 beat

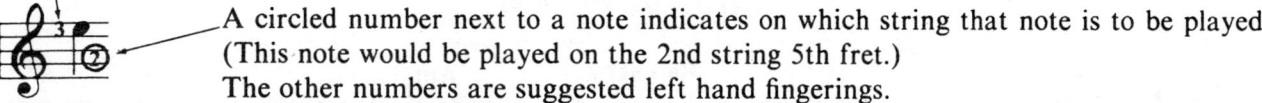
—If two notes appear to be on the same string play the bottom note on the next lowest string.
—Play this note on the 3rd string 4th fret.

left hand fingering

A circled number next to a note indicates on which string that note is to be played. (This note would be played on the 2nd string 5th fret.)
The other numbers are suggested left hand fingerings.

*Play the B note on the 3rd string in the 4th fret. Remember, the circled number indicates on which string the note is to be played. The other numbers are suggested left hand fingerings.

43

44 Playing Two or More Notes Together (Pick-Style)

Exercise 2

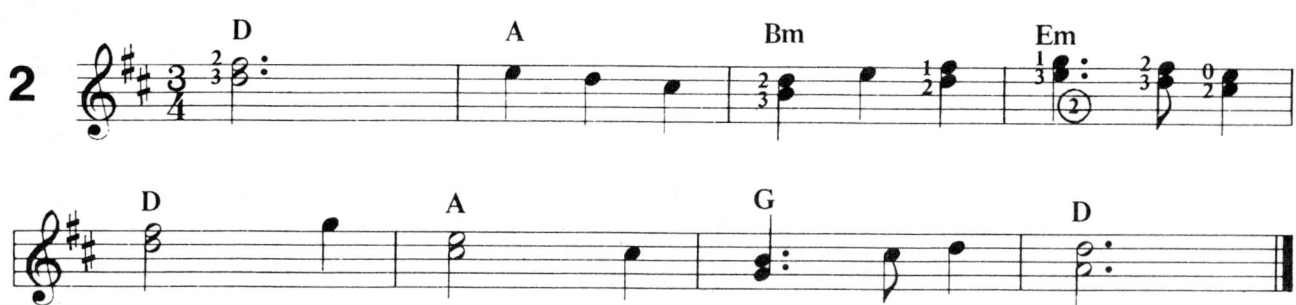

Shenandoah

Harmony for Corey

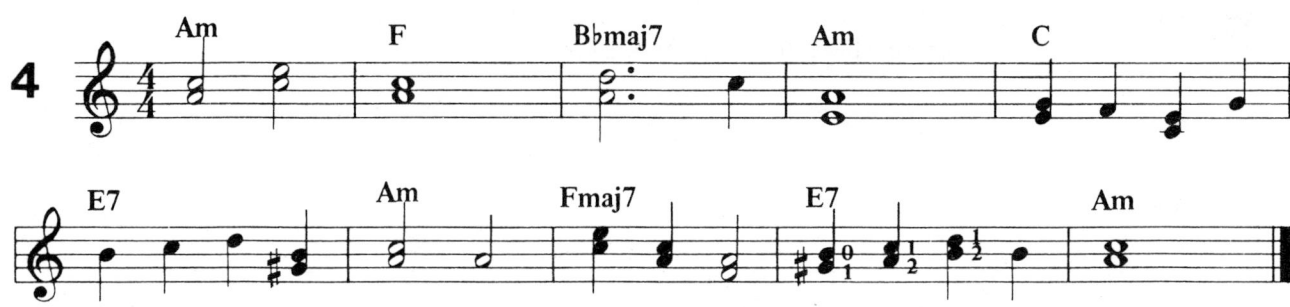

Playing Two or More Notes Together (Pick-Style)   45

MORE THAN TWO NOTES TOGETHER

A *chord* is three or more notes played together. Chords can be written as three or more notes stacked on top of one another. A three note chord is called a *triad*. To play a chord, begin with the *top* note and find where each note in the chord is located on the guitar, then play the notes of the chord together. Strike the strings quickly so they sound simultaneously.

The time value of the chord is the same as if one note was written. For example 𝅗𝅥 = 2 beats, ♩ = 2 beats

Play the following containing triads (three string chords).

Scarborough Fair

*Notice the lowest note must be played on the 4th string to make it possible to play the other two notes.

Down in the Valley

Exercise 3

46   Playing Two or More Notes Together (Pick-Style)

Play the following piece containing four string chords. Remember, find where the top note is played, then the next one below it and so on. The notes on the chord should sound at the same time.

Black Is the Color of My True Love's Hair   *Trad. English Air*

Play the following arrangement of Greensleeves which contains Five String Chords.

Greensleeves

Fermata: pause or hold

9
TABLATURE

The following method of writing music for the guitar is called **tablature**. A lot of guitar music is written in this manner. The six horizontal lines represent the guitar strings with the top line representing the first string. A number on the line indicates the fret in which to place a finger. For example:

Because 3 is on the fifth line down, a finger should be placed on the 5th string 3rd fret. O means play a string open. Two or more numbers on top of one another indicate those strings should be played at the same time. The C chord would look like this:

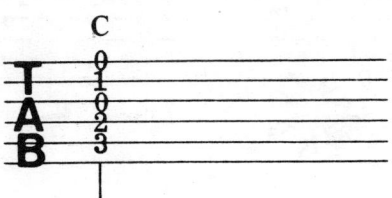

The stems on the numbers indicate the rhythms.
Ex. 6 = 1 beat, like a quarter note (♩).

6 4 = 2 to a beat, like eighth notes (♫).

Generally, the thumb will pick strings 6, 5, and 4. The first two fingers of the right hand will play the other strings. In 4/4, it is common for the thumb to play on the beat, similar to Travis style picking. The right hand fingering (p, i, m, a) is sometimes shown below or above the numbers.

Very often when learning an arrangement written in **tablature** much of what you will be playing is contained in the fingering of the chord which is written above the measure. For example, in the following arrangement of "Freight Train," hold a C chord to play the first two measures. Fingers may need to be added or lifted up (such as the first string third fret) but, most of what you will need is contained in the fingering of the C chord.

48 Tablature

Practice the following arrangements:

Freight Train
E. Cotton

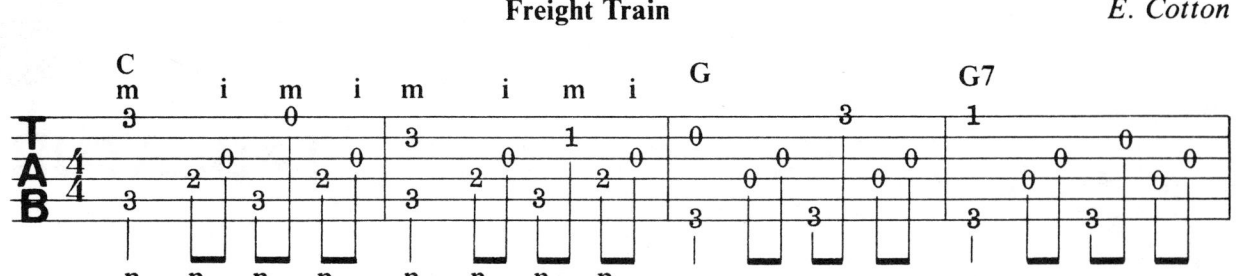

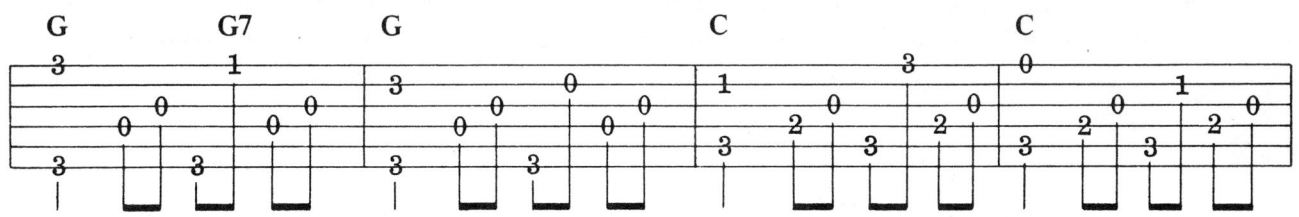

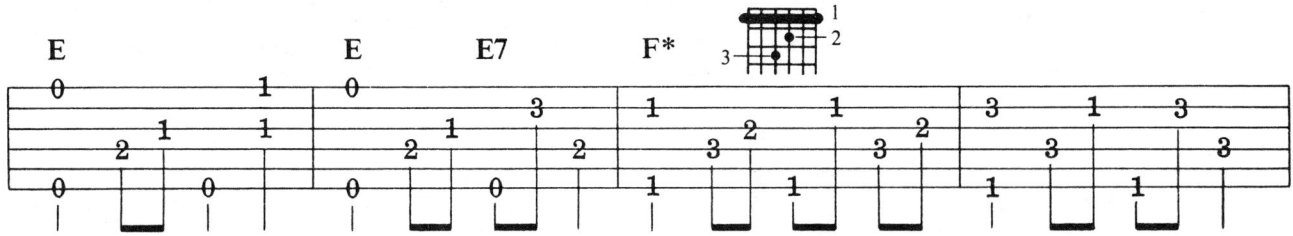

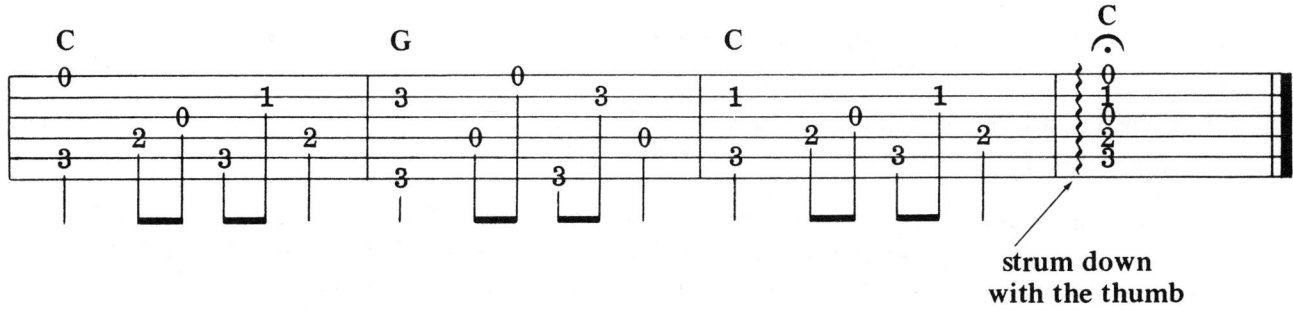

strum down with the thumb

*Use barre F.

Tablature 49

Wildwood Flower — *Trad.*

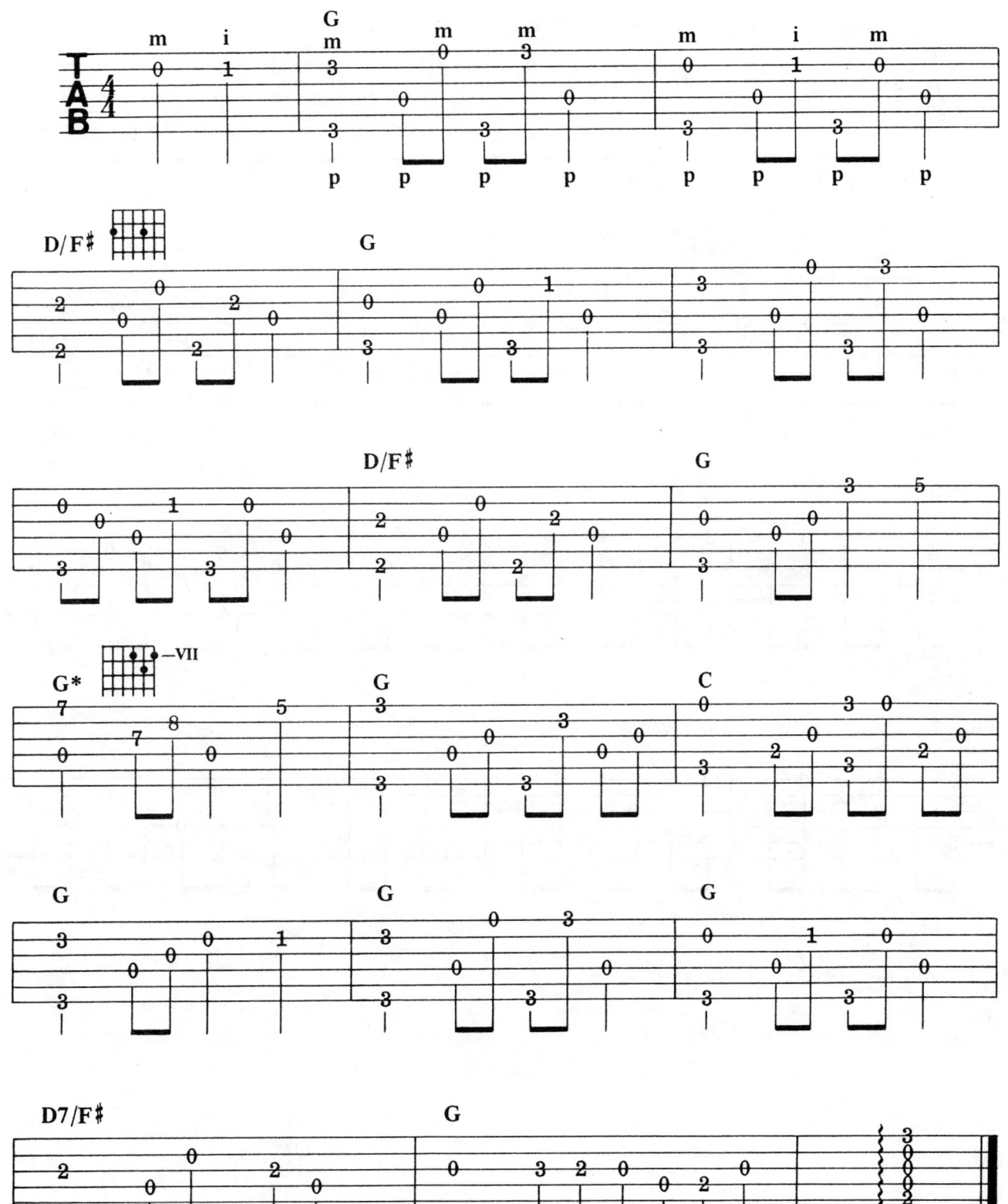

*This chord is played in the seventh fret (VII).

50 Tablature

Silent Night
Franz Gruber

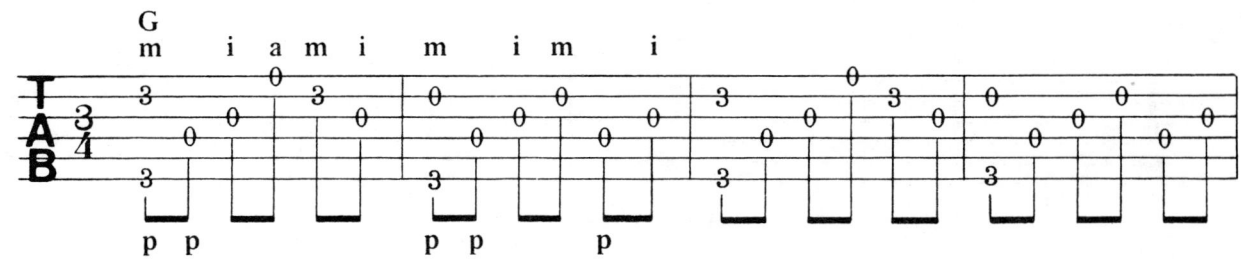
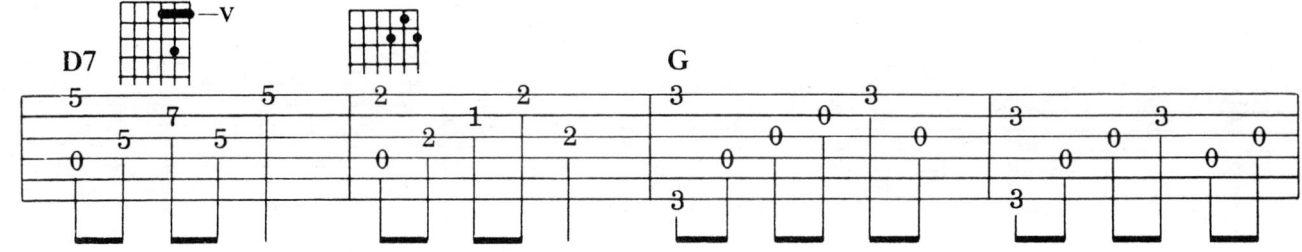
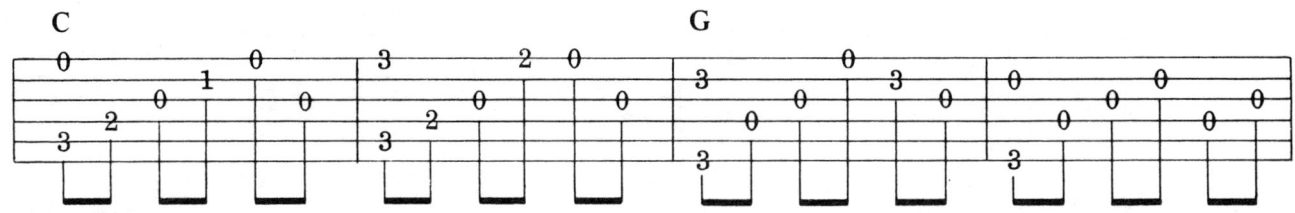
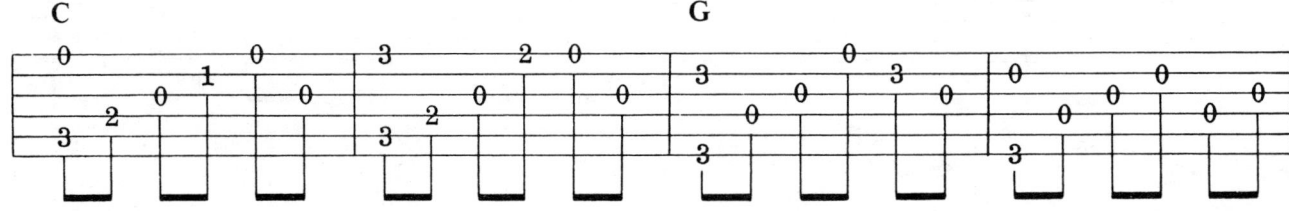

Tablature

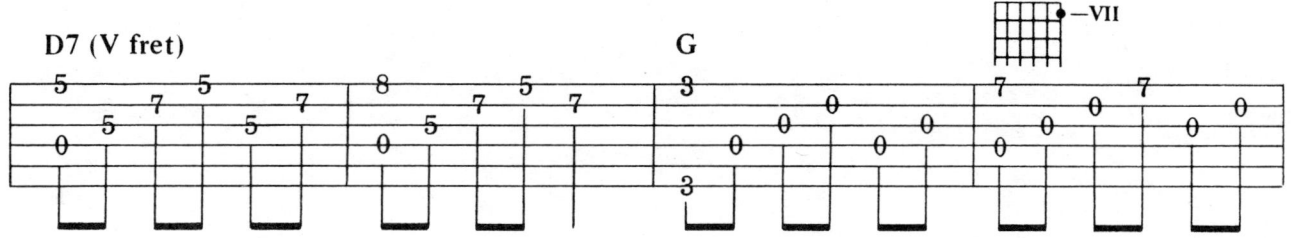

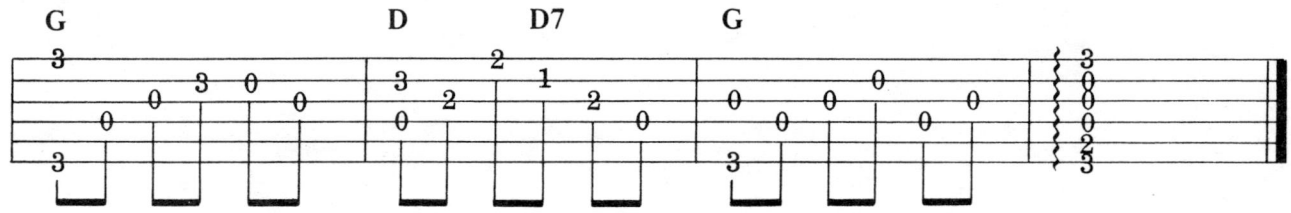

10
REVIEW

Practice playing 'Spanish Delight' using some of the skills you have developed. This piece should probably be played fingerstyle. It could however, be played using a pick. Notice the use of strum bars. If you are playing fingerstyle, the strumming in 'Spanish Delight' should be done with the first or first and second fingers of the right hand. Remember ⌐⌠ indicates to strum down-up.

You may recognize part of the melody as a Malagueña which is a traditional Spanish Flamenco style of music.

Review

*If you are using a pick, play the lower note with the pick and play the open E with the second finger of the right hand.

11
CHORD REFERENCE SHEETS

Major Chords

A	B♭	B	C	D
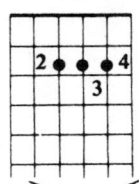	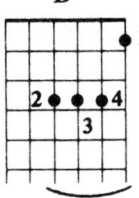	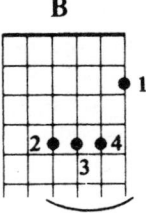	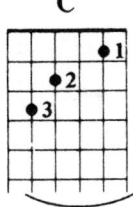	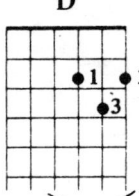

E	F	G
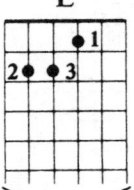	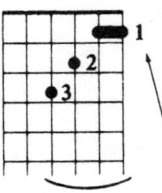	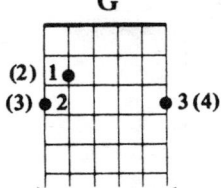

The first finger lays across two strings.

Minor Chords (m)

Am	Bm	Cm	Dm	Em
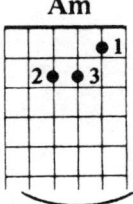	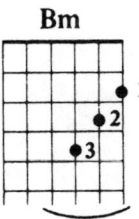	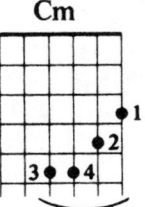	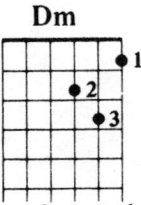	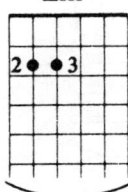

Fm	Gm
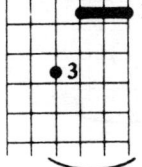	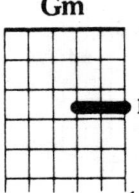

Chord Reference Sheets

Seventh Chords (7)

A7 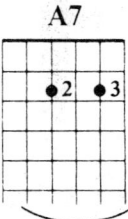   B7   C7 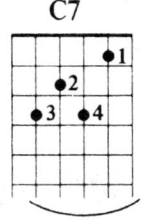   D7 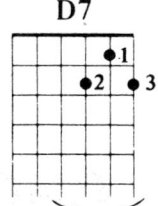   E7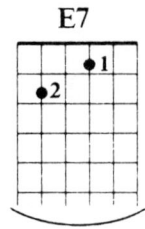

E7 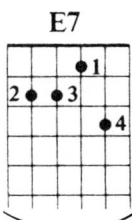   F7 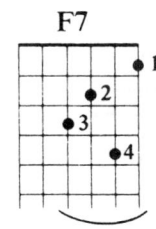   G7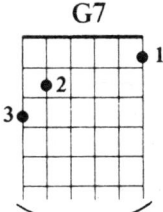

Major Seventh Chords (maj.7 – Major sevenths may also be written 7 or △)

Amaj.7   Cmaj.7 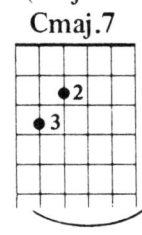   Dmaj.7 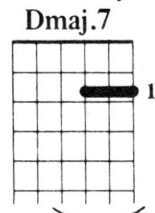   Emaj.7 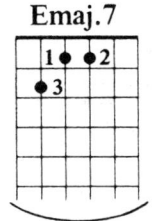   Fmaj.7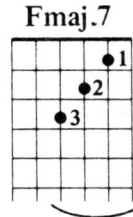

Gmaj.7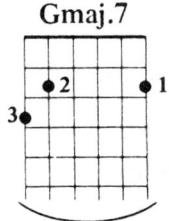

Minor Seventh Chords (m7)

Am7 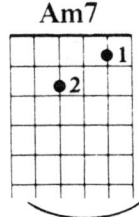   Am7 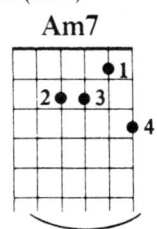   Dm7 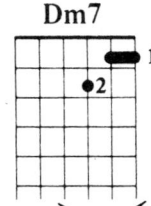   Em7 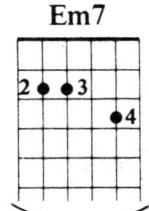   Em7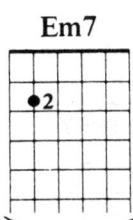

Chord Reference Sheets 59

Major Sixth Chords (6)

A6
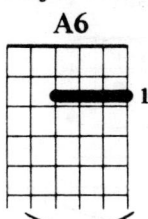

C6
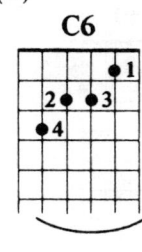

D6
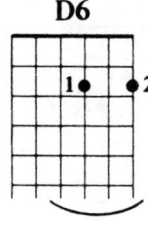

E6
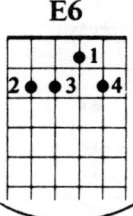

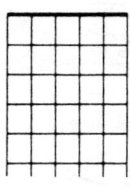

F6
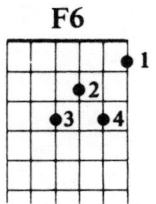

G6
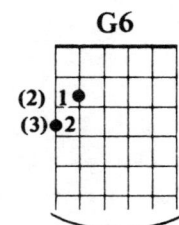

Suspended Chords (sus.)

Asus.
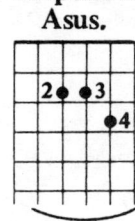

Csus.
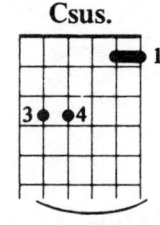

Dsus.
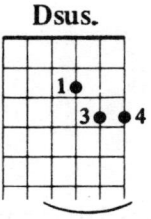

Esus.
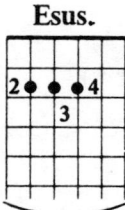

Fsus.
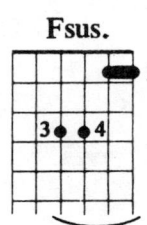

Gsus.
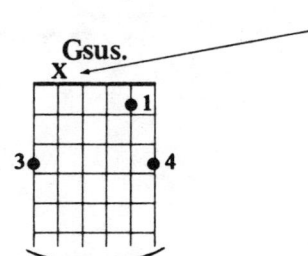

An x above a string indicates that string is to be muted (or deadened). This is done by tilting a finger which is pushing on a lower string (in this case the 3rd finger) and lightly touching the string to be muted. When the chord is strummed, the muted string should not be heard.

Seventh Suspended Chords (7sus.)

A7sus.
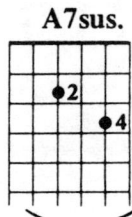

C7sus.
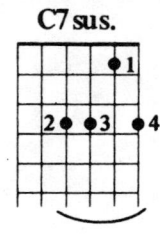

D7sus.
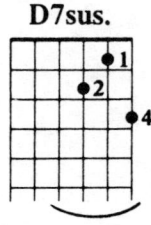

E7sus.
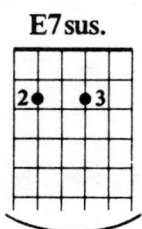

G7sus.
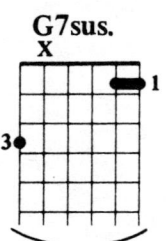

60   Chord Reference Sheets

Add Nine Chords (add9)

Aadd9   Cadd9   Dadd9   Eadd9   Gadd9

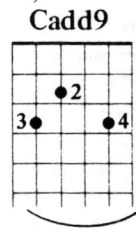
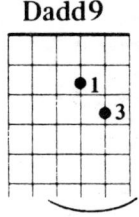
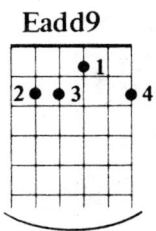
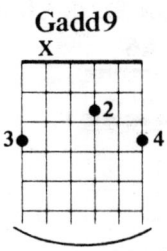

Diminished Seventh Chords (dim. or o)

Cdim., D♯dim., Adim., F♯°

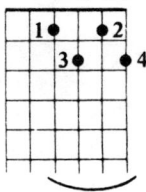

C♯dim., Edim., B♭dim., G°

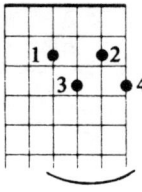

The diminished seventh chord can have four letter names for the same pattern. Every finger is on a note which names the chord.

Augmented Chords (aug. or +)
Faug., C♯aug., A+

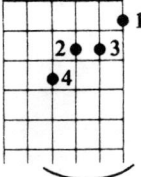

The augmented chord can have three letter names for the same pattern. Here again, each finger is on a note which names the chord.

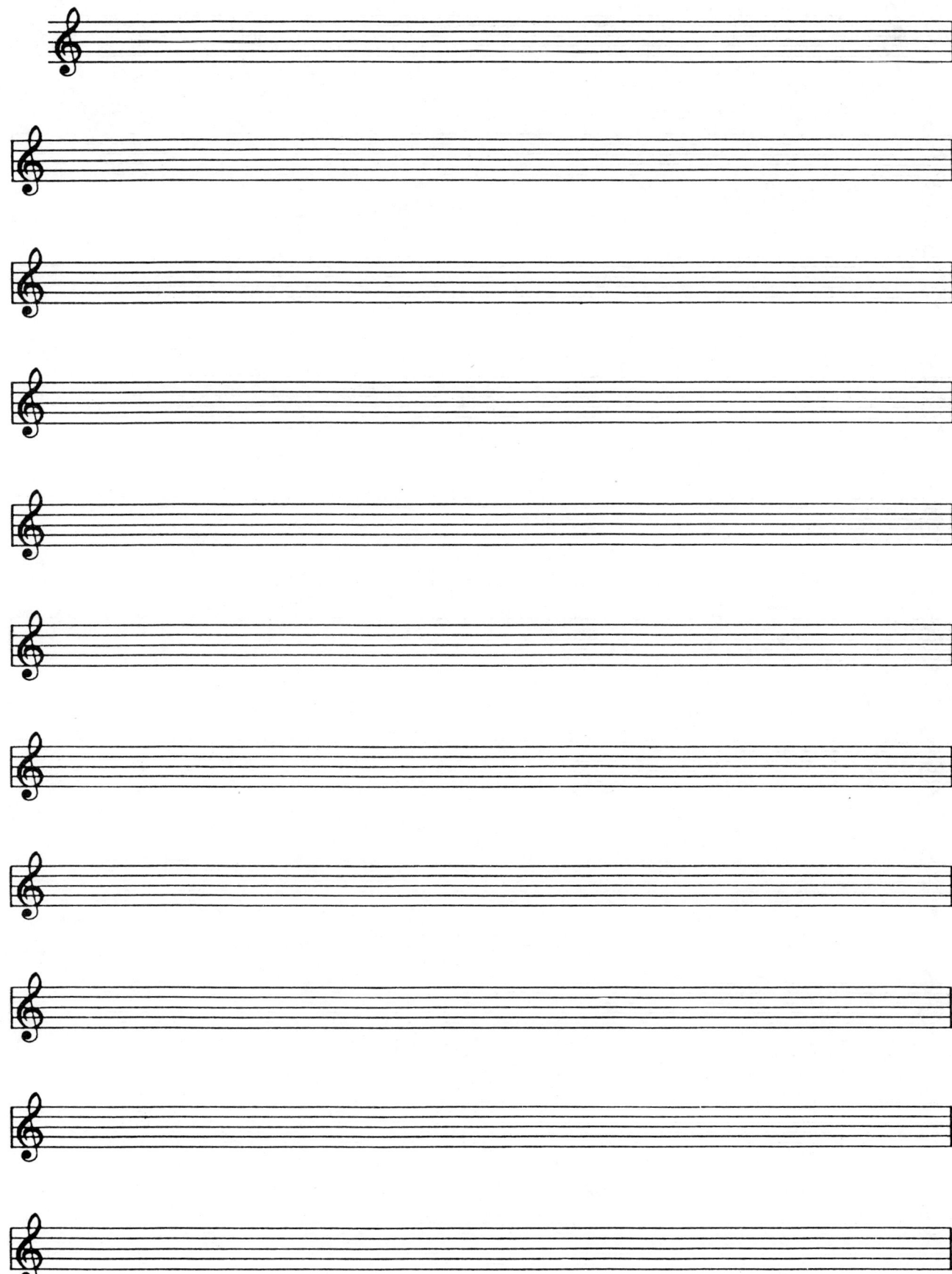

NOTES

NOTES

NOTES

NOTES

NOTES

NOTES

NOTES

NOTES